Fr. Paul

MW01491504

RUSSIA'S ERROR

Published by

MAETA
METAIRIE LOUISIANA

RUSSIA'S ERROR
TABLE OF CONTENTS

FORWARD

Arger Enterprises has offices throughout the world. As a result, it is necessary for me to travel extensively and visit many areas of the world, which I feel have a tremendous amount of internal conflict and possible external conflict with other neighboring countries.

There is no doubt in my mind that there is an increasing sense of world unrest. Despite preparation for celebrating the turn of the century, there lurks this *absence of peace* or sense of impending doom. Father Trinchard's book presents and explores areas of tension as well as reminding us of the God-given Marian solution to crises we now face and will increasingly face in the future.

G. J. Scholz
President
Arger Enterprises, Inc.

RUSSIA'S ERROR

TEXTUAL CONTEXT

This book contains the full message of my talk, which was given at the <u>Fatima 2000 Conference: World Peace and the Immaculate Heart of Mary</u> in Rome, Italy, on November 18, 1996. Most likely, Jesus was born in 4 B.C., according to the reliable research of historians and scripture scholars. Thus, providentially, the year of this conference was the two thousandth year after Christ's birth, perhaps a tacit sign of God's approval.

Immediately across (from the building wherein the conference was held) was the Basilica-- "The Home of Immaculate Mary, the Queen of Peace." This reminds me of the gospel passage usually read at most of the Marian Masses within the Canonized Liturgy of the Latin Rite (Jn 19: 24-28). Jesus said to John, *"Behold thy Mother,"* and from that moment he took her unto his home. The priest, John, was the one who created Mary's home. He did so through the Holy Sacrifice and Holy Sacrament, which he--not Our Lady, brought into existence. This reminds us that each church within which the Canonized Liturgy is said, was built as *Mary's home.* Here, the one who is identified as *the Lord is with thee dwells* with her Son, Jesus Christ.

Holy Mary is the Queen of Peace. Ultimately and essentially, peace is freedom from eternal Hell. The Fatima Message began, *"I am the Angel of Peace."*

The heart of the Fatima Message is Our Lady's concern for the salvation of souls in these most perilous times. This prophetic concern was evident in the climacteric Fatima Message given at Tuy, at which Sister Lucy was given the Great Salutary Theophany of the Holy Sacrifice of the Mass as our only salvation!

Thus are we led back to this Marian basilica--the home of the Immaculate One, the Queen of Peace. Within this basilica were the following words etched into the granite of the apse:

> *Nos concredimus ac consecramus tibi cordi tuo immaculato. Together with thee, we believe; and, we are sanctified through and consecrate ourselves to, thy Immaculate Heart.*

We believe unto salvation with the same faith which Mary had and which our Mother gives to the Elect among us. *Concredimus*--the Elect believe with Mary. *"Let all be done to me and by me as God decides."* Only by sincerely repeating and implementing Our Lady's response to God's revealed Will can one be saved from eternal Hell.

How are we consecrated or made holy? As each Angelus Prayer assures us--through the sufferings and death of Christ or through the Holy Sacrifice of the Mass. The primary *cause of* or *motivation for* the Holy Sacrifice is the only sinless human person--the Immaculata. The primary effect of the Holy Sacrifice of Christ is the salvation of the Elect from Hell.

Holy Mary--the Immaculata, is the only person who is totally obedient to God. Therefore, God loved her and bestowed upon her the great gift of being the *channel of all graces,* as the original Greek clearly implies and the root meaning of the Greek states. *"Hail, Mary, the channel of all (salutary) graces." (Lu 1:28)* The Immaculata *as the channel of all graces,* is *the human person* through whom salutary graces come.

Furthermore, in our time, Holy Mary is freely given to us by God as His prime end-times sacramental (Gn 3; Apoc 12). She will crush Satan's head in this, his most successful time. Through Holy Mary, peace will come to us--in time and eternally.

INTRODUCTION AND BACKGROUND

Russia's Error results from Man's rejection of God. It is the *rule of God-rejecting Man over men*, as opposed to the *rule of God as revealed over men*. Therefore, it existed since Adam's sin. However, it flourishes as New Age socialism today.

Some of the greatest and most important God-given messages to post-Apostolic times come to us through Our Lady of Fatima. Some of these Fatima messages concern the spread of Russia's Error (s) throughout the world until the reigning pontiff turns to God's freely given end-times sacramental--the Immaculata or the Immaculate Heart of Mary--and does *as God commands.*

Until the pope activates the Fatima Opportunity, we remain under the Fatima Curse. According to St. Thomas, a *curse* is *the state in which God allows greater demonic activity.* How does the Fatima Message present this curse--the dethronement of *God as revealed* and the enthronement of man as a god?

This cursed mind set will increasingly envelope the whole world. Man increasingly will be enthroned. *God as revealed* increasingly will be dethroned.

The Fatima Message also assures us that Russia will be used by God to punish mankind. Nations will be annihilated. The good will suffer. The existential church will become increasingly dysfunctional, as most likely was disclosed in the Third Secret. The Church was portrayed as being dysfunctional by the Fatima symbolism in the miracle of the sun which occurred on October 13, 1917. In this theophany, Our Lady restored the sun to its proper functioning. Worst of all, of course, is the God-disclosed fact that *many many* will go to eternal Hell while we live under the Fatima Curse, while the demons lead many into Russia's Error.

What is the Fatima Opportunity? This is the opportunity for the pope to consecrate Russia to the Immaculate Heart of Mary *as God requested at Fatima.* Then the Fatima Curse will turn into the Fatima Blessing.

Why *consecration to the Immaculata?* A significant part of God's revelation to us is that Our Lady is so *positively sinless* that she alone among human persons is totally transparent to Divinity. She alone is chosen by God to be the dispenser of all graces, as the great Fatima Salutary Theophany at Tuy in 1929 confirms. When one prays to Mary, as it were, one prays to God. When God favors us salutarily, He does so through the Immaculata. Our Lord Himself explained this to Sister Lucy, regarding why Russia must be consecrated to the Immaculate Heart of Mary: *"I want it known that all graces are granted through the Immaculate Heart of Mary."*

Why is *the required consecration* to be done *by the pope*? Only one man represents God to us and us to God. That's the pope. To a great extent, as he goes, so goes the church and thus, so go society and individuals--in time and for all eternity.

On July 13, 1917, Our Lady made certain requests of the Fatima children. She also told them that Russia was to be consecrated to her Immaculate Heart.

If my requests are heeded, many souls will be saved and there will be peace. The war will end. But if men do not cease offending God, another worse one will begin in the reign of Pius XI.

When you see a night illumined by an unknown light, know that it is the great sign given you by God that He is about to punish the world for its crimes, by means of war, famine, and persecutions

3

against the Church and the Holy Father. To prevent this, I will come to ask for the consecration of Russia to My Immaculate Heart, and the Communion of Reparation on the first Saturdays of the month.

If my requests are granted, Russia will be converted and there will be peace. If not, she will spread her errors throughout the world, raising up wars and persecutions against the Church. The good will be martyred, the Holy Father will have much to suffer, various nations will be annihilated.(The Whole Truth About Fatima, Frere Michael, phone:1-800-263-8160 to purchase).

Our only hope for reversing the Fatima Curse, under which we now increasingly suffer, is that the pope *consecrate Russia, as God demanded at Fatima.* At the conclusion of the great Salutary Theophany of the Tridentine Mass to Sister Lucy (June 13, 1929) God specifically requested the pope and his bishops to activate the Fatima Opportunity at this critical period in human life. **This consecration is so important because it came as God's application of the great Salutary Theophany at Tuy.**

The time has come when God asks the Holy Father to consecrate Russia to the Immaculate Heart, in

4

union with all the Bishops of the world, promising by this act to save her...I have come to ask reparation: pray and sacrifice for this intention.(The Whole Truth About Fatima, Frere Michael, pp 10-11)

The climacteric Fatima Message of 1929 completes the basic Fatima Message of 1917. It insists that *now is the time for Russia to be consecrated as God explained through Our Lady in 1917.*

FATIMA VALIDATED

All authentic Marian apparitions arc validated by God. One or more prophecies are made and fulfilled. The major validating prophecy of Fatima happened on October 13, 1917. Beforehand, God predicted sensational events, *which were perceived and thus, validated, by all present.*

Other validating signs occurred. However, let's consider God's prediction of World War II. On July 3, 1917, God revealed to His little children the following.

When you see a night illumined by an unknown light, know that it is the great sign given you by God that He is about to punish the world for its

5

crimes, by means of war, famine and persecutions against the Church and the Holy Father. To prevent this, I will come to ask for the consecration of Russia to my Immaculate Heart, and the Communion of Reparation on the first Saturdays of the month.

On the night of exceptional light, God will begin an event to punish us. World War II began on that night. Hitler saw this light on January 25th, 1938, when he determined to begin World War II.

If Russia were consecrated as God demands, then Russia is converted--made Catholic. There is peace-- the Reign of Christ--throughout the world. Many are saved. If Russia isn't consecrated as God demands, then Russia's Error spreads throughout the world. There is war, the good are martyred, nations are annihilated and the Holy Father will suffer much. Many souls will go to eternal Hell.

AN ERA OF PEACE

What is this *era of peace* that will be granted to humanity when the Marian pope activates the Fatima Opportunity? Three words stand out: era, peace and humanity. Our Lady indicates that she does not promise *merely* a *lull between wars.* In Portuguese, the words are *Algum tempo de Paz...* which is literally *some time of peace.*

The Vision uses the word *peace* in conjunction with the statement: My Immaculate Heart will triumph." Peace, therefore, means not merely the absence of conflict, but *the Reign of Christ*--the time when the Holy Sacrifice will flourish everywhere. The Angel who appeared to the children to prepare them for the visitations of Our Lady called himself *the Angel of Peace.* Only Christ -Sacrifice and Sacrament--is our peace, as all Church-approved Marian visitations have demonstrated.

God promises peace--not to Russia, not to the United States, not to Europe, but--*to humanity.* It will be a *universal peace,* a triumph of the principles of Catholicism. It will be, most probably, the greatest of all Catholic eras since it will be the universal Reign of Christ as King of His whole world.

Peace and reparation dominate the Fatima Message. From its very beginning in 1916, to its climax in the Great Salutary Theophany in 1929, peace has been one of Fatima's major concerns.

WHY 1917? WHY 1929?

On May 5, 1917, Pope Benedict XV asked Our Lady for peace. Perhaps, as a direct answer to his prayers, Our Lady began her appearances at Fatima on May 13, 1917. At Fatima, Our Lady disclosed God's Peace Plan for our times.

The chief antagonist to world peace also appeared in 1917. In November of that year, Russia was taken over by socialist-fascists. Also, in that same month, the Balfour Declaration created the Jewish state of Israel, thus beginning the time-clock for the end-times or the times of the Apocalypse.

In the same year, 1917, that the Fatima Message was given to us, God also gave us His freely chosen prime end-times sacramental--the Immaculata. As Russia and Russia's Error constitute the evil of the end-times. Our Lady and true devotion to her form the end-times sacramental--the God-given means to bestow special graces to us so that we can conquer Satan, even though we may be physically conquered. God's Providence was also shown by God's giving Sister Lucy the climacteric vision of Fatima at Tuy in 1929. Here, the Holy Mass was shown to be the true source of peace. The graces of the Mass come *only because of* and *through Our Lady.* Implicitly, at Tuy, God disclosed that peace will materialize through that Mass which was instituted by Christ and said by the pope, all bishops and all priests (of the Latin Rite) in 1929.

What else happened in 1929? Under Metropolitan Sergei Strgodorsky (1861-1944), the schismatic Orthodox Church became the apostate Russian (Orthodox) Church. Is this the Second Beast which supports the First Beast, Russia? (Apoc 13) Was this the urgency which led God to grant to us the Great Salutary Theophany and to make His urgent request for the pope to activate the Fatima Opportunity?

PEACE THROUGH REPARATION

The message from the Great Salutary Theophany focused on reparation. Our Lady concluded her message: "I have come to ask for reparation: Pray and sacrifice yourself for this intention." Peace will come to us through reparation.

The word reparation, was used in the Mass Liturgy of that day. *Reparation* meant *the full and positive realization* or *the fulfillment of God's justice--God's plan for us.* In its canonized Mass liturgies, the Church prayed that souls be repared by the gift of the Holy Sacrifice and Holy Sacrament (of the Mass). Here, then, is how the other closely related theme of Fatima is to be understood. Peace comes to us *through reparation.* Reparation brings peace.

The entire Fatima Message is directed to reparation- -in society, in the church establishment, and especially, in individual souls. Reparation is the restoration of God's *preferred Will* being done on earth. Reparation is the antithesis of Russia's Error-- the enthronement of man and the dethronement of *God as revealed.*

TWO FATIMA PRINCIPLES

As you may have already perceived, at least two principles are illustrated in the Fatima Message. Or, we could say, we are led to perceive (at least) two premises operating within the God-given Fatima Message.

Both are reflected in the Bible--especially Genesis and the Ne'vim, or Old Testament prophets. God reveals in Genesis that in His economy, *one* can represent *all*. This principle is employed in the Fatima Message. The pope is the vicar of Christ to men and the vicar of men to Christ. Since the pope represents mankind to God, we must conclude that as the pope goes, so goes the church and so go society and individuals (in time, as well as for all eternity). The pope is, as it were, the new *earthly* Adam.

As the pope chooses to disobey the Fatima Message, by refusing to activate the Fatima Opportunity, we continue to suffer under the Fatima Curse. Remember that the word *curse* is used as St. Thomas defines it: *God's granting greater freedom to the devil and his angels.* A few previous popes perceived the foreshadowing of the Fatima Curse. They dreaded this curse, as we shall see shortly.

There is another Fatima premise or principle--the prophetic pattern of history--as illustrated in the books of God's Old Testament prophets: Men are evil; God curses them; men continue to be evil, until (as it were) they hit bottom. Then, they confess their sins, repent, do penance and cry out for God's mercy. God pardons and blesses--only to have men fail again, some time later.[1]

Where are we within this prophetic pattern of history? So far, the present pope seems to reflect mankind in its rebellion against God. Fr. Malachi Martin contends that God may have appointed Pope John Paul II in order to have us come closer to *bottoming out*. However, what the reigning pope does or fails to do is determined by our prayers and sacrifices on his behalf. We cannot isolate and criticize the pope since, according to the God-given Fatima Message, the pope is *as we make him to be*. There, but for you and me, goes the truly Marian pope, the pope who will actuate the Fatima Opportunity. We are *not* in the era of Fatima Blessings. Instead, we dwell within the Fatima Curse.

EXTRA ECCLESIAM

In one of the last public and trustworthy official interviews allowed to her (December 26, 1957) Sister Lucy

---

For a further pertinent application of *the prophetic pattern*, consult Holy Mary Holy Mass, (available from MAETA). Here, St. John Bosco's predictions are analyzed and applied.

complained to Fr. Fuentes about the ever-worsening spiritual deafness and loss of faith. Sister Lucy stated:

Father, the Holy Virgin is very sad because no one pays attention to her message, neither the good nor the bad...Father, God is about to punish the world and He will do it in a terrible way...Tell them [the popes?] that the Holy Virgin said to my cousins Francisco and Jacinta and to me repeatedly that many nations will disappear from the face of the earth, that Russia will be the means used to accomplish the punishment from Heaven, if we do not succeed in the conversion of this poor nation...the devil is about to begin a decisive battle against the Virgin, and because he is capable of offending principally God and perverting in a short time the greater number of souls, he is doing everything in his power to gain the souls of the persons consecrated to God...Expect no call for penance from the Holy Father addressed to the entire world; and don't even let us expect them to come from our Bishops...It is now necessary for each one of us to begin, on his own, the spiritual reform of self. Each one must save not only his own, but all the souls that God has placed in his care. (The Whole Truth About Fatima, Frere Michael)

For the benefit of those who may still blindly trust ecclesial authority in a dysfunctional existential church, Sister Lucy (in giving her message) warned us *not to look to the pope or bishops for a positive reception of God's Fatima message.* We are *without the establishment's leadership.* However, it is up to us--Mary's remnant, to pray, work and sacrifice for the good of the Church, the world and individuals.

These are the worst of times. God and His Mother are ignored by the good and rejected by the evil. Satan is bringing many souls into Hell. The Holy Father and the bishops seem unconcerned.

PROVING AND REFUTING

As God disclosed to us at Fatima, until the pope consecrates Russia as He demands, Russia's Error will spread throughout the world and Russia will be used to punish the world for its sins. This message is not outdated. It's more relevant than ever.

Are we now in the era of Fatima Blessing? Has Russia been converted? Is the world at peace? Does Christ reign as king? Or, is the ecclesial establishment "lying" to us, as it assures us that the papal consecration of the world (not Russia) on March 25, 1984, met God's Fatima-given specifications for the consecration of Russia?

What actually happened on March 25, 1984? Pope John Paul II, in Rome together with some (not all) of his bishops throughout the world, *consecrated the world--not Russia, as demanded by God in His Fatima Message.* He alluded to the fact that he failed to consecrate *Russia,*(specifically by name), by praying in particular *"for those people who still await our consecration."* From the glasnost year of 1989, the ecclesial party line--not corrected by the pope-- insists that the consecration of Russia as demanded by God at Fatima *"has been done and done well."*

Briefly stated, let us demonstrate whether the God-bestowed Fatima Opportunity, perceived as having been activated, is in fact, activated--or *not activated-*-by proving or disproving the following syllogisms. It's a matter of simple and irrefutable logic regarding these two basic syllogisms.

If Russia were consecrated as God demands, then Russia is converted or made Catholic. There is peace--the Reign of Christ--throughout the world and many many souls are saved.

If Russia were NOT consecrated as God demands, then Russia's Error spreads throughout the world and there is war--NOT PEACE. The good are martyrred, nations will be annihilated, the Holy Father will suffer much and many many souls will go to Hell.

RUSSIA'S ERROR PERSONALIZED

Russia's Error is the *enthronement of Man as deceived and as deceiving* and the *dethronement* of *God as revealed.* Russia's Error exists in two modalities--*the diabolically feminine* and *the diabolically masculine.* In the moral realm, what is *not of faith* is *not of grace.* What is *not of grace* is *diabolic.*

God has commanded that each of us love Him totally and exclusively. Then we are to relate to or care for others *out of and according to the love of God--in agreement with*--God's Revelations in the Bible, in Apostolic Tradition and in all of the binding decrees of the Holy See or the Apostolic See, from St. Peter to the last binding or dogmatic papal decree.

The failure to hold or believe in *God as revealed* is of the devil (Ro 14:23). The devil and his angels lead us to disbelief or to unfaithfulness to *God as revealed* through their malice and snares, as the now suppressed Leonine (after) Mass prayers stated.

Many go to Hell. Why? We are under--what inside circles in Rome refer to as--the Fatima Curse. Here, you are reminded again, *curse* is used as St. Thomas defined it--*God gives greater freedom to the demons.*

Now, more than ever before, many of us are victims of these demons. Many are victims of Russia's Error--the enthronement of man and the dethronement of *God as revealed.* As we have seen, such a state was foreseen or predicted by saints and popes--especially, by popes. Also, as we shall see, such a state of affairs is increasingly materializing within our midst.

God does not leave us hopelessly under the Fatima Curse. He promises that we will live for some time enjoying the era of Fatima Blessings. We eagerly await the Marian pope--that pope who will activate the God-given Fatima Opportunity to consecrate Russia *as God specified in the Fatima Message.* God assures that this pope will materialize when enough of us are sufficiently praying and sacrificing for the pope.

TWO MODALITIES
ONE PSYCHOSPIRITUAL LAW

Satan disclosed his *game plan* in the book of Genesis, chapter 3. *"You shall be as god deciding good or evil"--"Eat of the God-revealed forbidden. It's nice and pleasant to your natural self."* Satan entices by diabolic deception. Sister Lucy of Fatima assured us that many of the clergy are under a diabolic deception. They are blind leaders for the blind.

"You shall be as god." That's the diabolically feminine modality. The psychospiritual law is that the diabolically feminine must degenerate into the diabolically masculine. The diabolically masculine is the rule of Satan by fear, force and other evils. The diabolically masculine is the fruit of being deceived by Satan. It's *hell on earth--a faint preview of coming horrors.* The diabolically feminine and the diabolically masculine are referred to as Russia's Error (s) in the Fatima Message. Russia's Errors can be reduced to what I call *Russia's Error--the dethronement of God as revealed* and the *enthronement of man as deceived and deceiving.*

More than ever before, *"the world lies in the lap of Satan (1Jo 5:19)."* Russia's Error has spread throughout the world. The Third Secret (a God-given revelation kept secret by the pope) most likely discloses that Russia's Error has invaded the church. Therefore, since Russia's Error permeates both the Church and society, Russia's Error victimizes many. Since this is true, Our Lady has assured us that *"many many go to Hell."*

Because of the awesome deception which prevails in our times, many of us need special help to see the truth about ourselves. I will try to show that, most likely, you are an unaware *victim of Russia's Error.* Grace builds on "nature." By God's special graces, may my natural remarks become salutarily (unto salvation from Hell) sanctifying unto greater life in Christ. Before we consider how Hitler and Marx fell under Russia's Error, let's consider how the demons tend to seduce us away from *God as revealed* to embrace man--what the Bible refers to as *"the world and the flesh."*

THE WORLD AND THE FLESH

In the diabolically feminine modality, one sins in order to be pleased--in order to live for his sensual, spiritual or social appetite. Living for or from one's sensual desires defines committing sins of the flesh. Living pridefully constitutes sins of pride. Adam ate of the forbidden fruit because it was pleasant. Also, *"eating the forbidden fruit"* promised that *"he would be as God (Gen 3:5)."*

Worst of all, Adam ate of the forbidden fruit to please man--to please Eve or to be validated by her, a sinner. *"She ate of the fruit and gave it to him and he did eat of it (Gen 3:8). "* Nothing of the flesh will enter Heaven (Ro 8:8; 13, I Co 6:9). No one *who lives to please others or to be pleased by others* can enter Heaven (Jo 1). Lastly, God resists the proud (1 Pe 5:5). He will not unite them to Himself for all eternity.

The diabolically masculine modality is a faint realization of Satan's kingdom on earth. As men abandon *God as revealed,* they become Satan's children. *Sin* is *missing the mark*--not living as God demands (Phil 3·14).

The diabolically feminine modality is characterized by self-satisfaction and pleasantness (at least, superficially). Here on earth, the diabolically masculine modality leads to personal frustration and hate disguised as love. Here on earth, the diabolically masculine arises out of hatred disguised as love and socially brings men into conformity to the reigning experts or authorities through fear and force. Now let's briefly consider how Hitler and Marx were diabolically feminine and diabolically masculine-- practitioners of Russia's Error.

21

DEFINING THE HITLER PHENOMENON

Ultimately, as St. Paul assures us (Eph 6:12), our warfare is against demons--evil spirits or evil focal points of thoughts and attitudes against God's Will. Being under the Fatima Curse, satanic principalities and powers assaulted Germany to produce Naziism-- the first major military national socialist form of Russia's Error. Nazi Germany was subsequently followed by Russia. Then, as predicted by Our Lady of Fatima, Russia's Error has now invaded China, the USA and other nations.

Let's learn from the past. Look at the formative period of Nazi Germany. **Nazi Germany, which was used by God to inflict Fatima's Curse upon mankind, had one of its sensual roots in aberrant homosexual behavior. One of its roots was in licensing and in actively indulging in God-forbidden sensual delight.**

According to the homosexual historian, Parker Rossman (Sexual Experience Between Men and Boys), an elite group dedicated to *"pedagogic pederastry"* was the basis used by Hitler to form the youth movement. Also, Abrams and Lively (Pink Swastika) have documented dozens of proofs that the whole *Hitler phenomenon* was rife with aberrant homosexual leadership. Of course, this is only the sensual aspect. Intellectually, Hitler was *proud*. He was obsessed with the occult and wanted to form a neo-pagan religion with himself as its major leader and object of worship.

To do so, Hitler ordered Himmler to formulate the basic doctrines of a great German neo-pagan religion--the Nazi New Age Religion--which would be imposed on Hitler's liberated victims. Such an ecumenical religion would be a blend of Germanic paganism, Eastern mysticism and Christianity, impregnated with Russia's Error. (The Twisted Cross, Joseph Carr)

Imagine how we would be living, had Russia's Error been imposed upon us according to the desires and imaginings of Hitler? You don't have to do much imagining--the USA is heading in that direction, not in a "God-ly" direction. As predicted, Russia's Error is invading the whole world, especially, the USA. The spirit of Hitler is alive and prospering in governmental, educational and communication areas.

A common spirit--the spirit of Russia's Error--seems to prevail. God is being dethroned and man--as defined by reigning experts and authorities--is being enthroned by ruthless tyrants.

SATAN'S PROUD CHILD

Russian Communism was launched in 1917 and flourished thereafter. Its founders, Marx and Lenin, seemed to have been led by *pride*. They wanted power, prestige and worldly success. They were predominantly *prideful intellectuals* driven to re-shape the public's perception of God, man and the world, according to their own natural and God-rejecting likeness and imaginings. Behind the scene, did Satan enable Marx to be successful? In the rites of higher initiation into a Satanist cult, an enchanted sword, which ensures success in this life, is sold to the candidate. He pays for it by signing a covenant with blood taken from his wrists, promising his soul will belong to Satan after death. In his poem, called "The Prayer," Marx wrote:

The hellish vapours rise and fill the brain,
Till I go mad and my heart is utterly changed.
See this sword? The prince of darkness sold it to me,
For he beats the time and gives the signs,
Ever more boldly I play the dance of death.

Since 1984 (the March 25, 1984 *"consecration"* of the world) or 1989 (Russian glasnost or perestroika-- the *"conversion" of Russia*), Communism has not been abjured. Instead, it has been expanded, so as to include the whole world. People in the world are now headed towards a one world under *man as deceived and deceiving* and not under *God as revealed.*

Will the church save us from this horror? The church is dysfunctional and the pope refuses to activate the Fatima Opportunity. However, God is merciful to those individuals who sincerely seek His mercy. At Fatima, God gave His Mother as the special end-times sacramental. If one listens to Mary, God will turn the Fatima Curse into the Fatima Blessing, at least, for us personally. Socially, when enough are sufficiently praying and sacrificing, then God will overwhelmingly grace the pope into activating the Fatima Opportunity.

In the meantime, each one's personal challenge is to avoid succumbing to increased demonic activity of the world and the flesh, and to become one of Mary's Remnant--to seek, believe in, love and witness to *God as revealed* through graces obtained by the Holy Sacrifice (cf. Apoc 12).

THE FATIMA CURSE ON NATIONS

Russia's Error is the enthronement of Man himself as god and the dethronement of *God as revealed*. Such a dethronement and antithetical enthronement is Satanic.

The *love of man* in Russia's Error opposes and defies a major biblical command--to love God (Christ) totally and exclusively. The Bible repeatedly condemns man's self-directed love as *love of the flesh* and *love of the world*. Such love is un-Godly because it prioritizes love for man as a god and promotes the subjection of man to others in an *un-Godly* way.

Historically, such love of man (defined by us as Russia's Error) is the basis for all of the governments of this century, which Fatima condemned. These governments embrace the *God-less* subjection or conquest of men--even of the whole world--as their goal. Who defines this goal? The God-less elite, reigning experts and authorities, decide, decree and enforce the programs, policies and rules of both evil ecclesial and evil societal bodies. This is accomplished by those who have rejected *God as revealed* as they are nice or mean.

When operating in the diabolically feminine modality, reigning experts and authorities display *niceness* as they validate, facilitate and fulfill God-less or natural sensual or intellectual goals. However, as the Council of Trent taught, each man is naturally deceived and Hell-bound. As this Council taught, man not only tends *naturally to choose evil,* but also to be deceived into *perceiving evil as good and good as evil* (Rm 1:14-2:4). Thus, the validation of natural man is sinful. Thus, many perceive that the *Council of Trent opposes the evil spirit of Vatican Two. It opposes that mind set which presumes or propagates that each is naturally good or a god.*

Natural man isn't a god. He's naturally a "dog"--a "dog" on his way to eternal Hell. The only hope of such a "dog" is the Holy Sacrifice and membership in Christ's Catholic Church, which alone has the Holy Sacrifice. *Extra ecclesiam, nulla salus.* Outside of the Roman Catholic Church, there is no salvation from Hell. Such a statement is a perennial dogma of Catholicism.

Being Catholic, the God-given Fatima Message

presumes and explains that *man naturally goes to eternal Hell.* The Fatima vision at Tuy portrays *God's grace and mercy--the fruits of the Holy Sacrifice--as man's only hope of escape from eternal Hell.*

In this century, two factors increase one's chances for going to Hell--wicked existential churches and wicked governments. Governments that embrace and impose Russia's Error bring many to Hell. Also, existential churches that govern so as to imply or teach Russia's Error--the enthronement of man and the dethronement of *God as revealed*--bring many to eternal Hell. The question must be asked: Is the evil spirit of Vatican Two the enthronement of Russia's Error within the Catholic Church?

How do evil churches and evil states attract victims? In their diabolically feminine modality, they appeal to man's unbridled sensual appetites or to his intellectual pride or to his social pride--to be validated by others. Men have forgotten the message from Eden. Therefore, Eden must be repeated. The forbidden is embraced by world leaders. All of us suffer, especially from 1917 on. Since 1917, states and existential churches have promised fulfillment and have delivered only frustration.

Evil states and evil existential churches have fallen for Satan's lie: *You, man, will be as God--deciding what is right or wrong.* More and more, nations and churches have abandoned *God as revealed* to embrace man, as God-rejecting men now decide man should be. In their diabolically masculine stage, these states and churches impose their God-less wills--as programs, policies and binding duty--upon their victims, who don't know, love and obey *God as revealed.*

Evil church bodies characteristically abandon eternal truth for strictly enforced transitory policies and decrees. They abandon Apostolic Tradition for living traditions which oppose the Christ-given Apostolic Tradition as stated and as explained by past popes in their dogmatic teachings. Evil men abandon the God-given Magisterium, as it dogmatically decrees and teaches that Christ must reign as King of all nations in the world. They have substituted an ecclesial or societal rule which opposes this God-given magisterial mandate. Such "God-less" rulers dominate others. They are *diabolically masculine.* As William Penn observed, we will be ruled either by God or by tyrants. While we remain subject to Russia's Error, we remain subjected to ruthless human tyrants.

HOLY RUSSIA OR CURSED RUSSIA?

The alleged "conversion" of Russia in 1989 (as a result of the alleged "consecration" on March 25, 1984, the beginning of the sixth glasnost) wasn't a conversion in God's or Fatima's sense of the word. Obviously, the propagandists who contend that the consecration of the *world* in 1984 was the consecration of *Russia as Fatima requested* are lying to us (deliberately or indeliberately).

Since 1984 or 1989, Communism has not been abjured. It has instead been expanded so as to include the New World Order. One ardent Communist has verified this. Mario Rodriguez, Cuban Ambassador to Italy, recently remarked:

> We do not abjure Communism. However, don't think by *Communism* I mean the stereotype one associates with the word or the very great errors which have been made in its name ("View From Cuba," Giovanni Cabeddu, 30 Days, No. 6, 1996)

In fact, *old Russia* and *new Russia* remain the same. They are both socialist nations. Socialism has been solemnly condemned by the Church. Popes have dogmatically decreed *that no one can be a socialist (or embrace Russia's Error) and remain a Catholic.*

Let's now evaluate contemporary Russia and its alleged conversion in greater detail. How has Russia been converted? Has it renounced the God-condemned Russia's Error? The answers lead us to key critical questions. *Has the Pope consecrated Russia as God instructed? Are we now in the reign of Christ? Has Russia become Holy Russia? Do we now enjoy an era of Fatima Blessings?*

The answers to these questions determine whether or not the reigning pontiff should still be strongly encouraged to activate the Fatima Opportunity. Also, they determine whether or not we should *ease up* on our prayers and sacrifices for the virtual *conversion* of the pope and for the actual conversion of Russia.

Lastly, our answers determine whether we should prepare for God's wrath or continue to enjoy God's ever-increasing blessings. Should we prepare for persecutions and annihilation of nations--or an ever increasing era of peace?

HAS RUSSIA BEEN CONSECRATED?
HAS RUSSIA BEEN CONVERTED?

If the Church approved Fatima Message is false, Fatima must be rejected. If the Fatima Message is true, and the pope has not activated the Fatima Opportunity to bring about an era of Fatima Blessings as promised by God, then we must act in urgency that the pope obtain special graces to activate the Fatima Opportunity.

God's Fatima Message states that *when* Russia is properly consecrated, the era of peace, the conversion of Russia to Catholicism, and the reign of Christ will follow. Since *none of the above* have materialized, we must conclude that the Fatima Consecration of Russia hasn't yet been accomplished as specified by God. It's a matter of simple logic, presuming, of course, that you believe that the Church-approved Fatima Message comes from God. Perhaps, we need to define and explain what is meant by *conversion,* since *conversion* is defined differently by those who contend that the Fatima Consecration has been *"done and done well"*.

SEVERAL CONVERSIONS

The ecclesial line, as reflected by Fr. Robert Fox, (and others), redefines *conversion,* as in *Russia will be converted...*to be *a change of heart.* In doing so, such propagandists optionalize the Fatima Message, blaspheme the Fatima Opportunity, and trivialize the era of Fatima Blessings. The definition of *conversion* becomes trite and loses its traditional meaning.

For those of us who have the Faith, *conversion,* as in *Russia will be converted,* means *conversion to the Catholic Church.* However, as an *"ad hominem* argument, we specifically inquire: Has Russia been converted to the Catholic Church? *How* has Russia been converted to the Catholic Church? *How* has Russia changed? This question can easily be answered from our vantage point--over twelve years since the alleged conversion took place.

1) Russia has converted from being a second rank military power to being the world's greatest nuclear power, thanks in large part to USA initiated programs such as START II and thanks to our leaders putting their heads in the sand. President Clinton repeatedly comments that *"There are no*

nuclear missiles pointed at the children of the United States tonight. " (<u>Washington Times</u>, "Coming to a city near you," James T. Hackett, Nov. 10, 1996)

Socialist Russia militarily is now over ten times more powerful than the USA. Each time one reads about an alleged Soviet disarmament, it is always to be accomplished at some future date or it is the phasing out of the obsolete in order to make room for the latest *state-of-the-art* weaponry--exactly as disclosed by General Lebed after the Gulf War.

At least, 25,000 nuclear missiles in Russia and China are pointed somewhere, and if not at the United States, *they can be retargeted in a matter of minutes.* On October 3, 1996, Tass reported *"the presidential button worked"* when a command from the *"nuclear briefcase"* triggered the launch of a ballistic missile from a Russian submarine in the Arctic Ocean. (<u>Krasnaya Zvezda</u>, Tass News Agency, as reported by <u>Washington Times</u>, James T. Hackett, Nov. 10, 1996)

For those with a modicum of intelligence, the only reason that Russia is so heavily armed is that it has awesome aggressive plans of conquest--not plans for peace. In another story on the same day, Tass reported that long-range bombers of the Russian Air Force ˙ unched two nuclear capable cruise missiles, which hit their specified targets. The report stressed the ability of the cruise missiles to carry their nuclear warheads 2,400 miles beyond the range of the bombers. (Washington Times, James T. Hackett, Nov. 10, 1996)

Remember, as poor Russians starve, *the state is building weapons at a pace close to that which America built weapons during World War II.* And, again we glean from the editorial page of the Washington Times:

> Extremely worrisome is the assertion [in the CIA's report of October, 1996] that command posts of Russia's Strategic Rocket Forces (SRF) 'have the technical ability to launch without authorization of the political leaders or the general staff' and that 'some submarine crews probably have an autonomous launch capability for tactical nuclear weapons and might have the ability to employ SLBMs [intercontinental ballistic missiles] as well.' (Washington Times, "Spinning away the nuclear missile threat, Nov. 10, 1996)

Indeed, we're more deeply under the Fatima Curse: *Russia will be used to punish the world for its sins. Various nations will be annihilated.* **Is not God now perfecting Russia as His instrument for destruction?** As reported in The Washington Times:

Both Mikhail Gorbachev and Boris Yeltsin have presided over the uninterrupted growth of Soviet/Russian military power. In 1995, cash-starved Russia spent close to $9 billion on continued production of the Akula II-class and the new Severedvinsk class of nuclear attack submarines, refitted all its Typhoon submarines with an upgraded version of the SS-N-24/26 ballistic missile, and embarked on the production of a new strategic ballistic missile submarine to replace the Typhoon. In addition, a new stealth fighter, three other tactical combat aircraft, and a new multi-purposed strategic bomber are being developed and produced. Finally, the development and production of chemical and biological weapons continue unabated. (Washington Times, "Russia bear not out of woods yet," Aug. 11, 1996, Miklos Radvanyi)

2) Russia is not converted. Russia causes wars and is now the most aggressive nation that ever existed. No matter how you define *conversion*, a converted nation does not plan to murder a large percentage of the world's population. In the past few years, Russia has sold submarines, tanks, planes and other military weapons to Iran. General John Shalikashvili, USA Chairman of the Joint Chiefs of Staff, told reporters that Iran had stationed very many weapons on islands around the straight, through which forty

percent of the world's oil supply passed. (Washington Times, March 1995, "Navies of Iran and Russia Worry US")

A converted nation does not spread wars. Therefore, Russia is not converted and the pope has not activated the God-given Fatima Opportunity. We all know what happens when anyone interrupts our oil supply. We now live in the era of the Fatima Curse--wars, famines, persecution of Catholics and an ever-increasing probability that various nations will be annihilated. We don't live in the era of Fatima Blessings--*world peace* and Russia's conversion to true Catholicism. Indeed, Russia will stir up wars throughout the world--exactly as predicted by God at Fatima. Such a scenario will prevail until the pope activates the Fatima Opportunity.

Georgie Anne Geyer, a popular columnist in Washington, observes:

"In virtually every case [of Russia's intervention in nations]--from Georgia to Tajkistan, to Azerbaijan--the Russians are going in to police conflicts they helped to create." (The Times Picayune, Oct. 19, 1994)

For example, the bitter struggle between Armenia and Azerbaijan in the early nineties, Russia supplied one side with aircraft and the other side with anti-aircraft guns. (Prophetic Observer, Dec. 1993) As an example closer to out times, Russia plans to sell 22 advanced diesel ships to China. (Washington Times, Mar. 7, 1995) Also, as we have seen, Iran has received modern submarines from Russia, setting off fears that it will target our oil supplies ships in the near future. (Washington Times, Mar. 19, 1995)

How did Russia create conflicts? In the recent past, it kept 100,000 troops in the Baltics against the wishes of the people living there. At Liepaja naval base, Russia housed a Libyan submarine, hosted and instructed over 100 Iranians on the use of their submarines, and trained naval personnel from Iraq and Algeria. (The Times Picayune, "The Russian Bear," John Metzler, July 23, 1993)

Why does Russia cause wars--exactly as predicted by the Fatima Message? In spite of propaganda to the contrary, most Russians reject the West and its ideals. Past Communist brainwashers or indoctrinators have successfully converted the present generation. "The perception of America as a hostile and weird place liable for all of humankind's troubles is deeply rooted [in Russia]." (Washington Post, "Thunder from Russia," Marat Akchurin, 11/92)

Even with the small amount of information that I've given, it should be obvious that Russia hasn't been converted--not even in Monsignor Guerra's (former head of the Fatima Shrine) sense of the word-- *"that men recognize that God really exists."* (Soul Magazine, 1993) Such a converted nation wouldn't make itself capable of destroying the world ten times over at the expense of the USA and of poor Russians. Such a converted nation wouldn't foment wars, for example, as reported in October, 1996:

> Kabul, Afghanistan--"Infighting between Taiban rulers and troops again threatened war-ravaged Kabul...refugees on Sunday reported heavy fighting...Taiban soldiers and government troops were pounding each other with tanks and heavy artillery fire." (The Times Picayune, "World Briefs," Oct. 21, 1996)

From whence came these tanks and heavy artillery guns? These came from non-converted (even to God) Russia, obviously! If the 1984 consecration were valid, Russia would no longer be God's instrument to inflict wars in the world. Instead, it would be at peace--within its borders and with the rest of the world. Obviously, the party line regarding the validity of the 1984 consecration is a party lie.

The only conversions of nations that can be perceived at the present time are of Russia becoming far more evil and of our becoming far more deceived. Lenin's evil tactics are successfully being deployed.

> Telling the truth is a bourgeois prejudice. Deception, on the other hand, is justified by the goal. When we are weak, boast of strength. When we are strong, feign weakness. (Vladimir Lenin, 1921)

3) The Russian people have converted to being *more sinful*. Now, they prefer the yoke of submission to the God-rejecting rule of men--to being free enough to seek the one true Church and to convert to it.

Russia has been converted--converted from being the evil empire to being an *ever more evil empire*. It is now more victorious over the *forces of good* than it was during the cold war. For example, since Russia's alleged conversion and granting of more freedom to Poland, the cold war's formerly *captive and Catholic Poland*, has become so wicked as to legislate murder by abortion--something the USA didn't do at the beginning of its subjection to the cult and culture of murder by abortion, since abortion was inflicted upon us by the Supreme Court.

Nearly all of the formerly captive nations of Russia remain socialist and thereby anti-Catholic. As The Wall St. Journal (Nov. 11, 1994) noted over a year ago:

> Of 22 countries that jelled from the revolutions of 1989 and the Soviet crackup of 1991, there are only four in which ex-Communists *aren't* in charge: Albania, Latvia, Estonia and the Czech Republic. They have 18 million people; the others have 358 million.(also Mindszenty Report, January 1996, "Quiet Return of Communism")

Russia's Error dominates the world, while Catholicism is in retreat. Russia's Error is intensifying within the hearts of most Russians. They prefer to be zooed animals rather than free humans. They are *"beating down the door, begging to be let back into their cages."*(US News and World Report, Nov. 1993).

They demand to be victims of Russia's Error. They refuse to commit themselves to *God as revealed.* Perestroika has been successfully employed to bring about greater evil. Soon, Russia will be as the people demand--*a zoo of caged humans.* (Ecclesial glasnost operates similarly.)

We must know and remember that the entire constitution of the Soviet Republic, both in legal

terms and practical matters, is based on the fact
that the Party does everything: planning, building,
and straightening out errors. (Lenin, 1929)

Pope Pius IX dogmatically decreed that no one can
be a socialist and a Catholic. The same can be said
concerning a communist, since communism is a
stronger form of socialism. The Russian people have
embraced Russia's Error and have rejected
conversion to Catholicism. The Russian people
prefer to trust in men rather than in God.

The Russian people hanker for the past, when you
had the illusion that someone--Stalin, the party
leader or your local trade union leader--was always
thinking of you; and your chunk of Kolbasa was
guaranteed, even if you had to stand in line for it.
(Time, May 27, 1996, p. 51)

Over three fourths of the Russian people strongly
desire *man-imposed* and *man-defined* order. (Time, May
27, 1996, p. 56) They prefer the zoo to the jungle. They
prefer *man* to God. In Russia, the Catholic Church,
which constitutes less than two percent of the
Russian populace, isn't recognized even as a
religious body.

'We have three officially recognized religions:

Orthodoxy, Islam and Buddhism' General Lebed said shortly before the July 3 (1996) presidential election. (Washington Times, "Archbishop fears surge in nationalism," Larry Witham, Aug. 4, 1996)

Furthermore, *Orthodoxy* as used by General Lebed and as referring to Russia, isn't orthodoxy. It's now the Russian Church--a church with an orthodox background and with an orthodox appearance, but a church body totally defined by the atheistic state. It's a contrived and well-regulated opiate for the people. Remember--the *Orthodox* Church become the *Russian* Church in 1929, the year of Fatima's Great Salutary Theophany. (Fatima Crusader, "What Happened in 1929?" Summer 1994)

God's words to Sister Lucy in 1929 assured her that this was the time to request the pope to consecrate Russia as God demanded. Since 1929 , leaders of the evil empire have successfully transformed the schismatic Orthodox Church in Russia into the Russian Church, similar to what key evil leaders are now trying to accomplish within the existential Catholic Church in the USA. Well over half of the alleged clergy in the Russian Church are KGB agents. (Catholic World Report, "Spies in Cassocks," April 1992)

The Russian Church has consistently condemned

Catholic proselytizing. This puppet of Communism has forbidden us to look upon Russia as being convertible. The leaders of the Russian Church do so in the name of ecumenism. The Russian Church stated that proselytism:

poisons the relationship among Christians and destroys the possibility of unity. These evil leaders chided 'certain circles inside the Roman Catholic Church for condoning such [missionary or evangelizing] activities,' since they are absolutely contrary to the spirit of dialogue. (Christianity Today, April 27, 1992)

Describing the *new and improved Communism*--which will soon be replaced by a more dictatorial ecclesial and societal regime--Alexander Solzhenitsyn observed:

The system that presently prevails is a combination of the old *nomenklatura*, financial sharks, fake democrats and the KGB [recently renamed the Federal Security Service]. I cannot call this democracy.(Time, 5/27/96).

4) In the widest (and "non-Fatima") sense of the word, Russia has *converted*. It has changed for the worst. In recent years, it has become more like the

USA, with its nearly five million violent crimes each year. Now, in Russia, gangs vie with one another to control everyday life. Typically, storekeepers must pay ten to twenty percent of their income to gangs-- or else.

Following the *consecration of the world in 1984*, (and not of Russia as Our Lady specified) we have not experienced world peace. We have experienced an increase in world crime. Russia has become the crime capital of the world. In 1993, Italy's Parliamentary Anti-Mafia commission (making progress against the Italian Cosa Nostra), made the startling announcement of a change of venue: *"The world capital of crime is now Russia."* (Mindszenty Report, Sept. 1994) Quite so, agrees Claire Sterling:

> There are over 5,000 organized crime gangs in Russia today and, at least 1,000 of them are known to be working with other foreign criminal groups. (Mindszenty Report, Claire Sterling, Sept. 1994)

Are these crime gangs part of the Fatima conversion and Blessing that God promised? If they are, most Russians despise and reject such "conversion." Most Russians prefer the old-time Communism to intensified crime and chaos. Russia has changed for the worst.

The Russia of 1996 is not just sick. In its current state, it is unreformable and thus lost as a humane society for the world. No country, not even the richest and most powerful one, let alone a morally devastated, debt-ridden and divided one like Russia, can stand so corrupt a political elite and successive governments for any length of time. For these reasons, people should feel sorry for Russia and the Russian people. And for the same reasons, governments, including the US government, must fear Russia. For Russia's continuing evasion of democratization and dogged pursuit of nuclear energy superiority will present an enduring strategic problem for the United States and the rest of the world. (Washington Times, "Russia not out of woods," Miklos Radvanyi, Aug.11,1996)

Recent Russian tactics have managed to dehumanize or "animalize" the people. Soon, they will have to be put back into their cages. That's why Gorbachev recently observed: *"Russia's Communists [sic] now demand a strict Stalinism."* (Time, 5/27/96). *Russia's Error--the dethronement of God as revealed and the enthronement of man as imagined and ruthlessly implemented*--remains as it was in the evil mentality that began to be imposed on the Russian people at the time of Fatima. The only difference is that the Russian people now willingly embrace socialism, (or neo-communism), which will be worse that classical communism because the masses freely embrace it. Russia has converted or changed from being a nation within which Russia's Error or socialism was imposed, to a nation which eagerly seeks or embraces communism. Russia has not been converted. Russia has been perverted. Now, Russia is far more evil than old or classical Russia.

In spite of propaganda hailing the end of Russian Communism, Communism is alive and well--as part of the New Age thousand points of light or as neo-Communism. This is shown in Gorbachev's words and in the very words of Cuba's ambassador to Italy, Mario Rodriguez: *"We are building our own way...without renouncing Communism."* (3o Days, "View From Cuba," No. 6, 1996).

It's obvious that the pope did not consecrate Russia as God demanded. When he does so, the Russian people will be converted to rejecting Russia's Error or communism. However, according to ecclesial propaganda, Russia has converted. *De facto,* it has (temporarily) converted to *Western decadence.* Perestroika has given way to *pornostroika.* The

47

people whose chains have been loosened have converted to living for the flesh. They have renewed and intensified their commitment to Russia's Error and thus, to Satan--not to God, and not to God's one and only true Church. Like a rebellious American teenager, Russia has rejected the old era of puritanical discipline and gone wild on pornography and drugs.

5) Russia has converted to being the most dangerous nation that ever existed--a nation at the mercy of "drunks and psychotics." One or two of these unstable people can easily bring about the annihilation of nations with even a small percentage of the 22,000 nuclear weapons that they could set off. Now, you can see how easy it is for the God-given Fatima Message to be fulfilled: *"Various nations will be annihilated."* Does this not verify that we are living under the Fatima Curse?

The October 1996 CIA report, labeled "top secret" was recently released. This report alarms us as it informs us.

> The disarray in the Russian forces is spreading to the elite nuclear submariners, nuclear warhead handlers, and SRF

[Strategic Rocket Forces].Russian officials themselves have asked for US help *"to ensure that 'drunks and psychotics' do not gain control of nuclear weapons."* The security of tactical nuclear arms...battlefield nuclear weapons...is very poor, according to the CIA, and *"these appear to be the weapons most at risk."* Russia has more than 22,000 tactical nuclear weapons. (<u>Washington Times</u>, Nov. 11, 1996)

In spite of awesome facts such as these, the party line is still being promulgated. Evil or duped Catholic leaders insist that Russia has been converted and that we are now enjoying peace--since, in their own words, the God-demanded consecration of Russia was *"done and done well"* on March 25, 1984. Even as they give reassurances that all is well, the sword of Damacles hangs over us.

6) Indeed, the Russian spiritual leaders have converted. Instead of embracing Catholicism, they have converted to being *more hostile* to the Catholic Church. The state-dominated Russian (Orthodox) Church has even issued a catechism, which goes out of its way to *"actually declare as being false--the primacy of Rome and the doctrinal infallibility of the pope."* (<u>Catholic World Report</u>, Feb. 1992)

There are ingrained ways of thinking that survive," says Adrian Karatnycky, president of Freedom House. "Communist leaders pay homage to religious beliefs as a means of exploiting religious fervor. For example, the return of an ex-communist in Poland will mean the opposite: looser ties between church and state. Kwasniewski has called for strict separation of church and state in the new constitution. (Christian Science Monitor, 12/6/1994)

Can this be the new Russia which the present and prevalent party lie assures us has converted to Catholicism? Obviously, the conversion that God promises *when the pope activates the Fatima Opportunity* hasn't yet occurred.

Interestingly, along with far less *orthodox* heretical sects, the Russian Church denies the Immaculate Conception. For them, Mary had to be saved from sin *exactly as we are.* Is this not why God demanded that Russia be dedicated to His freely given end-times sacramental, the Immaculate Heart of Mary-- the Immaculata? The Immaculata is denied by the Russian Church. Therefore, for Russia to be consecrated to her Immaculate Heart as Our Lady requests, our own uppermost clergy must *insult Russia and the Russian Church.* They must denounce, reject and make restitution for their (implementation of) sinful ecumenism. Remarkably, the first new Catholic church building was built about twelve years after Russia's alleged conversion. If such a fact means that Russia has been converted, we must hold that Rome has converted to the Muslim heresy, since it now has a mosque!

> "Christ the King Church, in Marx, is the first new Roman Catholic Church built in Russia since the communist revolution." (The Times-Picayune, New Orleans, LA.., J. Gallagher, 11/26/95)

Was the consecration of Russia in 1984 conducted as God requested at Fatima? If so, now--more than a decade later--Russia should be converted to Catholicism. Russia should be *blessed by God*--changed from cursed Russia to Holy Russia. Holy Russia should have many churches. Instead, only one Catholic Church was built in Russia by 1995.

Not only is Russia not converted, it is now *unconvertible.* The normalized (or compromised) state of the few Catholics in Russia is *that there be absolutely no chance of converting Russia. Who says so* is none other than establishment spokesman, Archbishop Tadeusz Kondrusiewiez, the apostolic administrator (not territorial archbishop) of Russia.

> We're in a *normal* situation. Catholics no longer
> seek conversions from other religions. Proselytism
> and expansionism are alien to us. We exist solely
> for Catholics residing in Russia. (The Catholic World
> Report, "Normal status in Russia," July 1996)

This leading propagandist for the acceptance of the
1984 *papal consecration of the world* as being valid
for the *consecration of Russia as God demanded* at
Fatima has now seen the light. In effect, he
acknowledges that not only is Russia not converted,
but also that *Russia can't be converted in the present
dispensation.* There you have it, as it were, from the
horse's mouth. Within the present stage of glasnost,
Russia is *forbidden to be converted.* It is now *under
"normal conditions."* It is now totally impossible to
convert Russia. Therefore, the consecration of 1984
was ineffective and not proper--to state the very
least.

7) *The world is not at peace!* There does not exist
an era of peace! Even the Holy Father confesses this
as *fact.*

> The world longs for peace and has need of peace.
> Yet wars...continue to reap innocent victims and to

52

cause divisions between individuals and peoples...In many parts of the world, whole nations are caught in the spiral of bloody conflicts...How can we fail to recall, in this regard, the bloody conflict between ethnic groups which is still going on in Bosnia-Hercegovinia? And this is only one case, amid so many situations of war throughout the world. (L'Osservatore Romano)

Even as the Holy Father confesses that we are not in an era of world peace, that wars are being fought, even this very minute (across the Adriatic and Mediterranean), he refuses to logically address the solution that he should fulfill Our Lady's Fatima Consecration request. Since we are not in an era of world peace, obviously, we are under the Fatima Curse--not the Fatima Blessing.

Again, the probability of Russia being used by God to punish the world has increased. For example, not only must we fear psychotics and drunks who have nuclear weapons at their disposal, we must also fear the leader of Russia. Recently, the President of Russia has been given the authority to initiate wars as he decides. The period of glasnost is coming to an end. Soon Russia will be worse than it was.

Yeltsin's new constitution (of 1994) *removes* checks and balances of preventing the Russian President from going to war.(Christian World Report, Feb, 1994)

Since 1994, the probability that various nations will be annihilated has increased, not decreased. Certainly, this is counterindicative of any sign that world peace will prevail. Also, *the pieces of the end-times puzzle* seem to be beginning to fall in place. Will Ezekiel's prophecy (Ez 38) concerning the invasion of Israel from the north (by Russia) come true?

In 1994, Yeltsin signed a mutual defense treaty with five predominantly Muslim, former Soviet republics. This set an ugly precedent, when one considers the rise of nationalist and neo-fascists, such as Vladimir Zhirinovsky, who have promised to restore the Russian empire.

I think we are seeing Ezekiel 38 set up right now...Russian leaders very much fear the Islamic fundamentalist movement in the five Islamic former Soviet republics...By treaty they are now obliged to be on the side of the Islamics in the next major Middle East war. (Christian World Report, Hal Lindsey, Feb. 1994)

There has been *no conversion to decent behavior*, and far less of a conversion to Catholicism. We should have suspected something was amiss when the alleged *revolution of 1989* was bloodless, compared to the Communist Revolution of 1917, wherein over sixty million were murdered, in order to bring classical Communism to maturity. Do not horribly bloody civil wars face the Russian people in the near future? According to General Lebed, a major political figure:

> Contemporary Russia isn't cut out to be a democracy. To restore order, Russia must undergo a bloody revolution. (U.S. News and World Report, 9/30/96)

8) Not only has Russia *not been converted*, it has duped nearly all of us into thinking it *has been converted*. Many mistakenly believe Russia to have converted to being Catholic, or at least, to have converted away from communism. Yet, it has successfully executed this perestroika ploy exactly as planned well over a decade ago.

A converted KGB defector discloses that a secret "Soviet collective leadership (since at least 1958) has been skillfully executing a theatrical display of 'democratism' designed to convince the West that a decisive 'Break with the Past' has taken place, in order to encourage Western Governments to abandon caution and to embark upon an open-ended program of collaboration with Russia [which will eventually turn against the West]. (The Perestroika Deception, Anatoliy Golitsyn, available from the Fatima Crusader: 1-800-263-8160)

Where are the Russian weapons intended for our annihilation kept? Nearly four decades ago, Nikita Khrushchev disclosed:

The Soviets intend to conceal vast 'reserves' of missiles and warheads, hiding them in places throughout the expansive Soviet Union where the 'imperialists' could not spot them. Later, they could be launched...in a nuclear war.(The Fatima Crusader, Winter, 1994, Nikita Khrushchev, speech to the Supreme Soviet, Jan. 14, 1960)

Today, it is conservatively estimated that the Russians still possess over twenty-two thousand nuclear weapons. This arsenal can blow up the whole world *eight times over.* Has Russia been converted or have we been deceived exactly as planned by the evil empire and its father--the father of lies?

Telling the truth is a bourgeois prejudice. Deception, on the other hand, is justified by the goal. When we are weak, boast of strength. When we are strong, feign weakness. (Vladimir Lenin, 1921)

Along with Satan, Lenin would be proud of his disciple, Khrushchev, and of other like-minded and similarly successful communists. Perestroika is *planned deception*, according to Mikhail Gorbachev.

Comrades, do not be concerned about all you hear about perestroika and our embracing democracy in the coming years. These are primarily for outside consumption. There will be no significant internal change within the Soviet Union, other than for cosmetic purposes. Our purpose is to disarm the Americans and to let them fall asleep. We want to accomplish two things: We want the Americans to withdraw conventional and nuclear forces from Europe. We want the Americans to stop proceeding with Strategic Defense Initiative. (The Fatima Crusader, Winter, 1994, Mikhail Gorbachev, speech to the Russian Politboro, Nov. 1987)

There you have it in *black and white*. The perestroika is satanic deception of the worst kind. The *perestroika ploy* will soon end. The sovereign state will reign supreme. To accomplish this, there will be a bloody purge. Millions of Russians will be murdered. Also, perhaps, nations will be annihilated--exactly as predicted by the God-given Fatima Message. With renewed vitality, Russia will become worse than ever and Russia's Error will more extensively and intensively spread throughout the world--especially, in the West.

As Fatima reliably foretold, Russia's Error--the enthronement of man and the dethronement of *God as revealed*--may have changed appearances. However, it will now invade and subject the world more than ever, until the pope activates the God-given Fatima Opportunity. In the remote past, Solzhenitsyn observed: "Americans are voluntarily Communists. Russians were forced to be Communists."

In Russia, this has changed. One of the greatest powers in Russia, General Lebed, assures us that now a great number of the Russian people yearn for the old regime, while millions of others have become accustomed to a *corrupt capitalism*. As we have seen, most Russians prefer the zoo to the jungle. These and other Russians will have to comply with the New Order or be murdered. Perhaps this New Order will include the USA and other nations as well. Perhaps this is how the New World Order will come into being and flourish--that is, until the pope activates the Fatima Opportunity.

The Fatima Curse has worsened. Now, both Americans and Russians yearn for an ever increasing rule of man. They both join together rejecting Christ as King, professing: "We have no king but Caesar. We will have no king but man." Now Russia's Errors are increasingly spreading throughout the world, as the New World Order materializes, in Russia, in the West, in China and throughout the rest of the world.

Cursed Russia, which was once under the hammer and sickle, remains cursed Russia. Now it is part of the emerging reign of the New Age kingdom of a thousand points of light. Russia is *not under the Holy Cross of Rome,* but under *a new and improved satanic Communism,* as well as under the anti-Catholic Russian Church.

CHINA ET AL

What we observe about Russia's strength could be stated about China's--perhaps, even more so. For example, as it secretly arms far above our World War II pace, it alone can fulfill God's Bible-given prophecy that an army of 200,000 will invade Israel from the East (Apoc 9:16; 16:12).

God's Fatima Message assures us that the acceptance of Russia's Error is the *primary cause* of present and ever-worsening future disasters. God's message also assures that the conversion of Russia will bring about world peace. China, Libya, Iran, Serbia, North Korea and other peace-deprived or hostile nations will enjoy a period of world peace *when Russia is converted.*

NEW AGE HEGELIANISM

"'Catholics have done two wrongs to Marx: contradicting him often for weak reasons, agreeing with him *always* for weak reasons.' Giacomo Contri, a psycho-analyst...seems to know what he's talking about. He has spent a great deal of time studying the beetle-browed father of Communism."(30 Days No. 2 1993)

Most are familiar with the Communist process of Hegelian dialectics. Thesis meets antithesis to produce a new thesis (synthesis) which, in turn, will meet another antithesis, and so on. Change, updating, revision, present understanding or current policy are some of the buzzwords employed within this process of New Age Hegelian dialectics.

Both Hegel and Chardin, the hero of Western Catholicism, believed in and advocated the practice of directed evolution as engineered by the reigning experts and authorities. In recent times, a slightly tempered form of Hegelianism has emerged--New Age Hegelianism.

SECULAR GLASNOST

The sixth Russian glasnost which began in 1989 and will terminate shortly (or has already terminated) employed New Age Hegelianism. The antithesis was engineered so as to be as Godless as the thesis. Thus, thesis, antithesis and synthesis remained within the New Age mindset--the mindset of Russia's Error.

The New Age is that belief system, religion or dominating religious spirit, which dethrones God and enthrones man on a worldwide scale. It does so both sensually and intellectually. New Age man lives to please himself or in servile fear of other men. His ultimate concern or religion is self-satisfaction or being subservient to *the world* (other humans).

Subservience to the world (or diabolically masculine rule by fear and force) happens when self-worshiping people form a village or are thrust into communal life. Then, one "god-force" must rule all the other "gods." Since God has been rejected and man is left with man, the only rule possible is the tyranny of man--being subservient to presently reigning authorities.

How do God-rejecting liberals rule? As in Naziism,

Russian Socialism, Chinese Socialism and New Age Catholicism--with force and fear. Thus, we enter into the diabolically male phase of Russia's Error (of socialism or of the New Age)--that phase which was born out of the blood of over 60 million Russian people in Russia and out of the blood of well over 200 million Chinese in the Republic of China and that will be born our of the blood of two billion people worldwide--according to New Age experts.

Being inconsonant with nature as created and designed by God, such man-rule periodically breaks down. In Russia, immediately preceding 1989, the year in which the sixth glasnost began, a diabolically masculine government ruled through fear and force. In 1989, Russian leaders successfully began to employ the New Age Hegelian dialectic. *Niceness* temporarily replaced *meanness.*

The soon-to-be-established sixth glasnost synthesis will be achieved in a New Age way. Having left God for man, the people remain unconverted. The Russian people have not even been allowed to convert.

This is the New Age secret ingredient. **The Russian people have been kept unconverted.** They have never been given the opportunity to convert. *They have been dumbed down to living for their flesh and the world.*

When temporarily released from diabolically masculine tyranny, the formerly enslaved hunger for order and fulfillment. Having not been allowed to convert, these Russians have only one hope--to return to their enslavers. The Russian people will return to their zoos not only to be fed regularly, but also to be protected from the enemy without.

Even now, most Russians fear and hate the USA and Europe more than the dictators within Russia. A most conservative and reliable source of Russian truth, <u>Pravda</u> stated: *"We will be ruthless to our enemies and our orthodox saints will approve."*
(<u>Pravda</u>,Yuri Vlasov, July 17, 1992)

I predict that a militant fascism greater than any previous one will soon engulf Russia and its enslaved satellites. Already, over 90 percent of the *freed Russian satellites* have voted to become enslaved--have voted to be ruled by communist or socialist dictators.

OUR PRIMARY CONCERN

Because of the ever-worsening condition of Russia, the Fatima Message leads us to realize that the state of the existential Catholic Church must be our primary concern. Let's recall two pertinent Fatima facts. First of all, God tells us at Fatima that as the Church goes, so goes the world or so go nations-- especially, Russia.

Also, in the often forgotten words of the Great Salutary Theophany at Tuy in 1929, God tells us *"I have come to ask reparation."* What needs to be repared in our day? As recent popes have stated and as classical saints have predicted, primarily the church establishment needs to be repared, to be brought out of its self-destructing modality (as Pope Paul VI confessed it was), and be restored to its *par--* as defined by Christ and as implemented up to 1960.

Some sensible Catholics are waking up. For example, James Likoudis perceives *new church (*in its pursuit of ecumenism and in its modernized *"popular entertaining and not very tasteful"* liturgies), as presenting insurmountable obstacles to its own favorite pursuit of ecumenism. Obviously, the number one task within the Catholic establishment is to repare itself--to come back to being *as Christ intended it to be.* (<u>The Wanderer</u>, "Ending the Byzantine Schism, James Likoudis)

THE MAJOR SOURCE OF RUSSIA'S ERROR

"Russia's Error will spread throughout the world"--God's Message at Fatima. Why? The existential church has betrayed God.

The Vatican-Moscow Concordat was an agreement between Russian leaders and the "powers" within the church of Vatican Two. These Catholic leaders agreed that the existential church would befriend Russia, Russia's Error and socialism. For some time, we lacked substantial confirmation that such a betrayal really occurred. Now we have such confirmation by <u>Inside the Vatican</u>.(Sept. 1994, pp 20-21) Cardinal Willebrands (then a monsignor) disclosed that he represented the church as he met with top Russian leaders in Moscow in August, 1962. They agreed to the following:

> No particular political system of governing will be named specifically...likewise, the question [of atheism] will be mentioned only within a whole system of problems now facing the Church-- problems such as witnessing to the truth and spreading the gospel...nothing that could offend

the Russians would be mentioned in any of the final texts [of Vatican II]. (Inside the Vatican, Sept. 1994, pp. 20-21 quote from Cardinal Willebrands at his meeting with Russian leaders in Moscow in August, 1962)

As we have seen, the Great Salutary Theophany at Tuy (in 1929) promised an *era of peace.* In Portuguese, this phrase connotes the universal reign of Christ, and thus, the worldwide reign of the *repared Church--that Church, which returns to Apostolic Tradition,* as defined by the unperverted Bible and the dogmatic decrees issued by *fully pope-ing popes* in all periods of Church history.

THE GOOD WILL BE PERSECUTED

Until the pope activates the Fatima Opportunity, we suffer under the Fatima Curse. This Fatima Curse is characterized by the persecution of good people or of the just. The *just* are those who live in a way acceptable to God or as Catholics should live. Obviously, faithful Catholics are persecuted within establishment churches in the West. One has only to open the files of any chancery. Good and holy seminarians are dismissed, orthodox priests are persecuted; and, legitimate complaints from faithful Catholic laymen are ignored. Increasingly, especially in the USA, traditional Catholicism is also being politically persecuted. It is being persecuted into compromise or silence. *The good are martyred* as Fatima predicted. In many locations, the world is not at peace. Catholics are being persecuted or murdered, according to information in Catholic World Report, (July 1993), which I summarize:

Since 1992, integrist Islamics have deported or slaughtered well over a million Christians in Sudan. In Mozambique, Nigeria, Somalia, Angola, Ethiopia, Mauritania, Uganda, Libya and other parts of Africa. Catholics are singled out for persecution and execution by integrist Islamics and others. Such anti-Catholicism agitates fanatic persecution of and intolerance toward Catholics in Iran, Saudi Arabia, and other places in the Middle East.

Throughout Latin America, we have hot spots of persecution, such as Cuba and Peru. Across the Adriatic Sea, Catholics are persecuted by the Serbians in what was once Yugoslavia. China, North Korea, Malaysia, Bangladesh, Pakistan and Vietnam actively persecute faithful Catholics. (Catholic World Report, July 1993)

Russia's Error, along with persecution and murder of

good people, afflicts the entire world. The hammer and sickle predominates, not the Crucifix.

PERSONAL CHALLENGE

Become convinced that evil will become more evil, in your own life, until you raise your fist in its ugly face and yell "Away with Caesar! I will have Christ totally rule me. Away with Russia's Error--the dethronement of *God as revealed* and the enthronement of man as defined by God-hating reigning experts and authorities."

Pray, work and suffer for the pope to embrace the God-given Fatima Opportunity: to consecrate Russia as God desires and to repare the existential church so that Christ's era of peace--Christ's Catholic Kingdom--may materialize upon the face of the earth for a period of time. Thus, it will be made easier for people to save themselves from eternal Hell.

THE NEXT TOPIC

According to the Church-approved God-given Fatima Message, when the pope and his subservient bishops consecrate Russia to the Immaculate Heart of Mary as specified by God, then Russia will be converted and an era of world peace and the reign of Christ through Catholicism will envelope the whole world.

We have seen that none of these results have materialized. Therefore, we must conclude that the papal consecration of the *world (not Russia)* on March 25, 1984, was neither valid nor acceptable to God.

UNFOLDING THE MYSTERY OF INIQUITY

Since the Fatima Message focused on Germany as well as Russia, we could study <u>Mein Kampf</u> to attain a deeper understanding of Russia's Error and the procedures used to implement Russia's Error. However, I leave that to you. Instead, let us consider Beria's talk (or teaching document) in Russia, 1932. Beria was head of the Russian KGB.

This chapter is crucial to bringing you to the conviction that we are in the Apocalyptic end times-- at least, in spirit. Satan is Lucifer--the light-bearer or *the mind.* Unlike nearly all of our intellectuals, Satan is eminently practical. Because of his wise combination of theory and technique, Satan is also eminently successful.

In Beria's talk, Satan's theories and techniques are presented on *a kindergarten level.* The least you should do is to grasp Satan's theories and techniques on this level--if you are to avoid being his victim and if you want to be motivated to do all you can by your prayers and sacrifices to lead the pope to do as Fatima requests. This is the age of Satan as well as the age of Our Lady, the Woman of the Apocalypse. Become ever more familiar with Satan's techniques. Know his working philosophy. Otherwise, you will easily become one of Satan's victims.

Beria's major Russian document discloses Satan's plan for the New Age, or Satan's plan to create and sustain the USA and other nations as socialist or New Age nations. Also a major directive from the People's Republic of China focuses on Satan's program for existential churches.

We will study the high points of these two crucial documents. We will also show how they are being successfully implemented--especially, in the USA--to create and sustain both the First and Second Beasts (Rv 13)--in spirit, if not also in fact.

All is progressing as planned. Russia's Error--the New Order--is spreading throughout the world in church and state--just as predicted by God in His Fatima Message. Now, in the nineties, is the time of Satan's greatest triumph socially and ecclesially. The Apocalypse is *now*. Until the existential church is repared, we suffer Apocalyptic horrors.

Satan is using his master plan revealed in 1932. He, the genius of evil, has revealed his plan in this important document. Become convinced that his plan as disclosed over sixty years ago in 1932 is now being implemented. Consider and apply the following points given in the talk by Colonel Beria of the KGB to young Americans at Lenin University in 1932. (Beria's talk--obtain a copy from The Foundation, POB 1009, Grant's Pass, OR 97526.)

BERIA'S TALK

I.   Russia's Error constitutes Satan's greatest assault against humanity. Russia's Error is God dethroned and man enthroned. *Man enthroned* **is** *the political arrangement of a sovereign state elevated to a position of authority over man and God's church.* **Satan has disclosed to us his specific plans on the implementation of his New World Order.**

Even though Beria's talk is elementary, it is inspired by the genius of evil. Let's see what the Light-bearer, Lucifer, plans for this world. Let's understand him as best we can since our lives depend on such knowledge.

Goals of the State should be formulated by the State for the complete obedience and concurrence of individuals within that State. (Beria's talk, 15)

Remember, Russia's Error is simply God dethroned and man enthroned. As the state (or God-displacing man) is enthroned, Satan himself is enthroned (Apoc 13).

A pseudonym for *man enthroned* is *the sovereign state*--the state in the place of God. The underlying premise within Beria's talk is that all allegiance, all obedience is owed to the state or to man and thus, to Satan. Man--*the reigning experts and authorities*--must dominate all people. As people allow man to be enthroned, they make themselves *slaves of the state,* which is Satan's great *evilmental*--that which emanates from evil and that which leads us to evil.

What increasingly determines the goals and morals of American citizens? The *sovereign state* or the *reigning God-denying experts and authorities.* Simply stated, as God is dethroned, man--in the form of reigning experts and authorities--takes the place of God and becomes a ruthless and tyrannical god who regulates our lives. This is true from regulating or determining what you can eat, drink or smoke to determining what you can say or even think. Even now, basic freedoms are being stripped away as government regulations proliferate--for example, in defining hate-crimes so as to punish *fundamentalists,* as ruling powers within the state arbitrarily decree.

Man (especially in the form of presently *reigning experts and authorities)* rules. As man rules, Satan rules, because *God as revealed* has been deceptively misrepresented and rejected. We are cursed with the rule of man as satanically deceived, cleverly deceiving and ruthlessly dominating.

Even now, government regulations are becoming so satanic that they are blatantly contradictory. For example, *one must not discriminate against homosexuals* (50% of whom tend to molest children); yet, as a pastor, one is *liable for employing a homosexual* who *does his own thing* on a child in one's congregation. Our government edicts and contradicts itself. Why? Satan is the father of lies.

However, you may contend that the American bishops will save us from all harm. Not so. At their worst, these bishops are part of the problem. At their best, these bishops are ineffective. They've lost their clout. For example, on the few occasions that they protested against abortion, they refused to call it *murder*, (since they believe that the State defines murder, not God); and more significantly, they *failed to speak and act authoritatively as bishops*. On the other hand, when as bishops, they wanted to impose *sacrilege* (communion) *in the hand* upon their flocks, they *acted authoritatively as bishops!* They forced each priest to give three sermons of indoctrination promoting sacrilege in the hand.

Why didn't they *act as bishops* regarding murder by abortion? Is outlawing murder of less significance than enforcing sacrilege? Have they already sold out Christ to the highest bidder--the Sovereign State? Many other examples could be cited. From all of them, we are led to conclude that the American bishops will not save us from becoming worse victims of Russia's Error.

We have seen the goal of Russia--to impose its error upon all men. What is the source of Russia's Error? Obviously, Satan is. We know God's Fatima prophecy--that Russia will spread error throughout the world, that it will be a worldwide dictator and that various nations will be totally annihilated.

Satan's thinking and methodology are disclosed by

Beria in his 1932 talk. (Remember Fatima's main message came on October 13, 1917, one month before the Russian Revolt). Our Lady came to inform us about Russia's Error, as well as, the only way to conquer Russia's Error.

II. Russia's Error leads individuals to live for or from the Community. New Age Catholicism, believing in Russia's Error, inspires and cooperates with the like-minded pervert-engineers of the USA. God is replaced by man.
Truth is replaced with the politically correct. Tradition gives way to experiential feelings and to blind obedience to one's leaders. Thus, are the minds and hearts of the presently victimized brought away from God into Satan's kingdom.

The individual is to live for the community, as defined by reigning experts. In effect, so teach most or nearly all religion books in the USA. And so teach governmental pervert-engineers. Eventually, those individuals who do not live for the community will be eradicated. Beria refers to such nonconformists as germs and wicked viruses, as follows:

> In any State we have certain individuals who operate in the role of the virus and germ, and

these, attacking the population or any group within the population, produce, by their self-willed greed, a sickness in the organ, which then generally spreads to the whole.

The constitution of Man as an individual body, or the constitution of a State or a portion of the State as a political organism are analogous. It is the mission of Psychopolitics first to align the obedience and goals of the group, and then maintain their alignment by the eradication of the effectiveness of the persons and personalities that might swerve the group toward disaffection. In our own nation, where things are better managed and where reason reigns above all else, it is not difficult to eradicate the self-willed bacteria that might attack one of our political entities. But in the field of conquest, in nations less enlightened, where the Russian State does not yet have power it is not as feasible to remove the entire self-willed individual. Psychopolitics makes it possible to remove that part of his personality which, in itself, is playing havoc with the person's own constitution as well as the group with which the person is connected. (Beria's talk, 7)

Can you understand this *elementary level* statement of Beria as given in 1932? Psychopolitical techniques are employed to achieve two of Satan's major negative goals--the first of which is to downplay, deny and not permit any victim to discover his own infinite dignity as an individual person, who in his moral choices to obey or disobey God, determines his own eternal destiny. Satan's other negative goal is to prevent his victims from discovering and encountering *God as revealed*--especially, the Holy Sacrifice and Sacrament.

Satan's positive goal is to lead each to live for and adore *man as god*, as self-gratifying or as the enslaving *community*. The adoration of *community*, which characterizes New Age Catholicism, is nothing more than a fundamental tenet of Russia's Error. Some of us can recall the pre-eighties trials in Russia where the *People's Court* or the community tried each individual as the reigning experts and authorities decreed, of course.

New Age Catholicism accomplishes Satan's primary positive goal by presenting a positive and affirming posture towards self-gratification, as well as by preaching community ad nauseam--in its religion books, sacramental programs and homilies. New Age Catholicism accomplishes Satan's primary negative goal by *trivializing* and thus, trashing,

Roman Catholicism, which holds such truths as "Extra ecclesiam, nulla salus" and that one must love God totally and exclusively. *Such teachings* are considered by New Age Catholicism as being *heresy* or such classical dogmatic phrases are twisted into insignificance.

Psychopolitics, as enunciated by Beria, was crude. Today, it has been refined into an art-science that is efficiently executed beyond our reasonable projections. I will cite one example of what is in store for our future under Russia's Error. Indeed, as Our Lady predicted, until Russia is properly consecrated, Russia's Error (s) will spread throughout the world. *Think globally* is the Novus Ordo Seclorum motto. Indeed, Russia's Error will define the global village or community.

The main item on the agenda for the Executive Council of the World Health Organization is the renewal of the health-for-all strategy. Being 'intrinsically population-based, i.e., focused on the needs of whole populations' [of the community] the primary health-care approach is essentially a matter of public health; this approach does *not* center on the health of individuals, but considers the overall health of communities. In 1992, Nakajima declared that we were 'still far too attached to providing the best possible health care to individuals, to the detriment of public health-care measures that would benefit the entire community.' (Catholic World Report, "Inventing New Ethics," M. Peeters, July 1996)

By the way, to insure the health of the world community, planners are determined to murder at least two billion people. What's in store for dissenters--for those who dare to question, resist or reject *the community's* decision, such as, to force euthanasia upon one's mother or father? Those who preach and impose the cult of man, or the tyranny of fascists are well prepared to handle dissension.

The interruption of a State goal will be discovered to have been the work of a person whose disloyalty and disobedience is the direct result of his own misalignment with life. It is not always necessary to remove the individual. It is possible to remove his self-willed tendencies in order to effect an improvement in the goals and gains of the whole. The technologies of psychopolitics are graduated upon a scale that starts somewhat above the removal of the individual himself, concerning itself first with the removal of those tendencies that bring about his lack of cooperation. (Beria's talk, p. 16)

In Satan's kingdom, those who acknowledge and obey *God as revealed* are misaligned. New Age Catholicism is Satan's best tool in the USA. It employs Satan's techniques *in the name of God*. It is the realization of end-times horrors--the Second Beast, which gives total approval to the First Beast. (Apoc 13)

Psychopolitical manipulation is ruthlessly applied in seminaries and in "Catholic" schools throughout the USA. In retreats, cursillos, discussion groups, Renew, RCIA and other church-meetings, psychopolitical manipulation of the group by the reigning experts and coordinators is manifest to all who can see. Outcome-based education is subtly leading the unwary to hold and vote to implement *the politically correct* in opposition to the *eternally true*. God is replaced by man: ("What do you think? How do you feel?"); or, by the politically correct *living traditions,* as defined by the community--the reigning experts and authorities.

III. Dumb-down individuals. Eradicate any and all allegiances to God-given Truth. Then, zoo the animal-men.

"We de-personalize and dispossess you for your own

good and for the community's good." This is the party line as preached by both evil churchmen and evil statesmen. Dumb-down and zoo. That's the agenda of the New (World) Order. Dumb-down into blind anti-Christ conformity. That's the agenda of the ecclesial Novus Ordo.

That's Satan's greatest victory--to lead his victims to renounce *true* religion in the name of *false* religion. Satan can rule only if the masses are reduced to being "pious God-rejecting" animal-men. Then, they will need the state and New Age religion in order to live. Each must be led to abandon living for Christ and His Will, especially, as revealed in the Bible and Apostolic Tradition--in order to make him dependent on contemporary political correctness as held by New Age religious leaders.

Each must be stripped of personality and of possessions so as to make each one dependent on the *sovereign state* or the *anti-christ church* for the basics of life. Then God fades away. Can you read through the double-speak in the following quote? You should be able to do this, if you're an aware *victim* or an aware *survivor* of the false or evil spirit of Vatican II. De-personalizing and dispossessing you "for your own good and for the community's good" is the party line as evil churchmen join evil statesmen in depriving you of God-given truth in the name of man-deceiving satanic lies. Today the existential church and the sovereign-state are executing the will of Satan on earth (as predicted in Apoc. 13) and as previously elucidated.

It has been said, with truth, that one-tenth of a man's life is concerned with politics and nine-tenths with economics. Without food, the individual dies. Without clothing, he freezes. Without houses and weapons, he is prey to the starving wolves. The acquisition of sufficient items to answer these necessities of food, clothing, and shelter, within reason, is the natural right of a member of an enlightened State. An excess of such items brings about unrest and disquiet, as well as independence from the sovereign state. The presence of luxury items and materials, and the artificial creation and whetting of appetites, as in capitalist advertising, are certain to accentuate the less desirable characteristics of man.(Beria's talk, 12)

Reduce human subjects to being dependent on the sovereign state for their basic needs. Render them incapable of independent existence. While this goal is being accomplished within nations, accomplish this goal globally. Convince each man to *think globally* and to will peace--peace as this world defines it--without beliefs, without guns with which to defend oneself, without possessions (about which fights begin), without distracting religious beliefs, without fundamentalist churches, etc. All such things prevent the state from becoming our god. Therefore, they must be outlawed.

"Imagine" is the theme song for getting the people of this planet to voluntarily embrace, promulgate and be enslaved to Russia's Error:

> *"Imagine no possession,*
> *no Hell to avoid*
> *no heaven above the skies,*
> *no guns, no beliefs to fight for...*
> *Then, the world will live as one."*

In the final analysis, man is to need only the God-less church and state as savior. All other loyalties are to be purged from him: loyalty to *God as revealed;* loyalty to do as one wills within proper God-given bounds; loyalty to one's primary family; and loyalty to one's social environment (as loyalty to friends and neighbors). All is as planned. Russia's Error(s), as spelled out in 1932, are now being implemented.

In rearranging loyalties we must have command of their [our victims'] values. The first loyalty [of every man] is to himself as defined by God--responsible and able to know, love and serve God as He wishes. This is destroyed by demonstrating errors to him, showing him that he does not remember, cannot act independently nor can he come to know God. The second loyalty is to his family unit, his parents and brothers and sisters. This is destroyed by making a family unit socially and economically dependent [upon the sovereign state] by lessening the value of marriage, by making an easiness of divorce and by raising the children wherever possible by the State. The next is to the State and this, for the purposes of communism, is the only loyalty that should exist once the state is founded as a Communist State. (Beria's talk, 12.)

Remember, Beria stated this in 1932. He disclosed Satan's exact Plan for the Novus Ordo. Such Satanic strategy has not changed. It has been implemented successfully in our times both in our nation and in wicked churches. Most American "Catholics" no longer believe in the Bible as God's infallible Word, or in the Catholic Church as defined by totally binding papally proclaimed dogmas. All of these satanic goals have been implemented in the USA by the evil state with the help of evil churchmen.

EVIL AMERICAN CHURCHES

Consider the American churches. Do not certain American churches excel in imposing (in spirit, if not also *de facto)* Russia's Error using the methodology disclosed by Beria in 1932? What has the Second Beast of the Apocalypse accomplished?

1) After abandoning the Bible as the sure conveyor of God's Word and the Catholic Faith as being a definite set of truths from the past church--leaders left each person without any sure foundation to "trust himself." Thus, each victim was led to abandon Apostolic Tradition and binding papal Tradition to embrace presently propagandized *living traditions.*

In Renew groups and elsewhere, each was led to follow the community (discussion group) and those who pre-decided what the communities should both discuss and conclude by how they were allowed to discuss: for example, no one is allowed to say, *"I must believe that practicing homosexuals are sinners who if they die in the state of mortal sin will go to eternal pains in Hell,"* because this is an essential Catholic Truth.

2) Evil churches--through their priests and other teachers--have destroyed the family and replaced family with themselves and/or the state.

For example, New Age Catholic student-victims are subtly led to see their parents as being merely care providers. Schools as defined by the state can become the morals provider. Church-supported classroom sex-indoctrination takes over the parents' right and duty, in this most intimate and private matter--both to impart information and values.

As it rides roughshod over the child's modesty, church-supported and church-imposed sex education as it exists in the USA, teaches the child that he *need not accept his parents' values* or *the traditional and binding teachings of the Church.* At first, in the diabolically feminine stage of Russia's Error, the child is led to think and feel that his own (apparently self-determined) goals and values are correct since he has formed them (usually with the *approval of the community).* In the inevitable diabolically masculine stage of Russia's Error, each child is indoctrinated (by force and fear) into considering himself to be primarily *a part of the community.* As such, he is expected to submit his mind, heart and behavior to the community--as defined by reigning experts and authorities who have dethroned *God as revealed* and enthroned man as imagined or imaged. (Apoc 13)

See how existential churches have betrayed even natural law--that each parent is the first and most important educator of his child. Concerning this delicate subject area, parents, by how they live and believe--never pre-programmed school teachers--are to promote and safeguard modesty and to impart sex knowledge prudently to each individual child. After all, whose child is this? Is it the state's--the village's--or the parents' child?

See how the state has taken advantage of parents in this most delicate area at this most precarious time of life for a child. Of course, once the USA inevitably goes into its diabolically male phase "Victorian morals" will be imposed--as they were in pre-1989 Russia and as they will be imposed in post-glasnost Russia. The *caring* state must degenerate into the *dominating* state--not only as regards sex, but as regards all other moral areas of life.

"Russia's Error (s) will spread throughout the world"--God's Fatima Message. The USA has faded away. We are now in the USSA, the United Socialist States in America.. When the USSA enters its diabolically male stage, we'll find the State as a permissive *feminized* parent metamorphasized into the tyrannical *male* parent. Such devolution is inevitable. The diabolically feminine *must degenerate* into the diabolically male. We will either be ruled by *God as revealed* or by tyrannical men.

Evil churchmen, instead of rightly pointing out Russia's Error and refusing to become part of this heinous scheme geared to the destruction of the Faith, have actively imposed Russia's Error: rejecting binding Catholic tradition and insisting that all children in Catholic schools receive this evil sex and life indoctrination, which they, with demonic deception, label *family life education, pro-life education, death education, health education, or even chastity education.*

Why do so many *religion* classes teach children that the best they can hope to become are citizens of a global community? Look at nearly all "religion books." *Community* is repeated *ad nauseam.*

After catering to man by dethroning *God as revealed*, the contemporary American church ruins "Catholics" for marriage as designed by God. The American church grants wholesale annulments, or in effect, easy divorces, as any honest chancery "marriage-breaker" in America will tell you. With such a prevailing church-engendered attitude towards marriage, how can any normal boy or girl enter marriage as defined by God or by the Catholic Church?

Since Russia's Error dethrones God, it must eradicate true religion and anything close to true religion. In the end, Satan can reign only when the purity and totality of God's revelation is destroyed-- both in preaching and in praxis. Paradoxically, today many evil churchmen help to accomplish Satan's goal--to destroy the Catholic Church as it was prior to the sixties--one, holy, catholic and apostolic.

One must believe *God as revealed* or one will be cursed to believe in and be subject to *man as imagined and man as imagining.*(Gn 3) Eventually and inevitably, there exists no other choice. Some bishops have more than done their part in spreading Russia's Error by destroying belief in the faith and morals (social as well as liturgical) of the Traditional

Church. They do so because they are under the Fatima Curse. They have lost the full and pure Faith. The "faith of our fathers" embarrasses many bishops in our day. They are embarrassed about the past, since it condemns many of them for failing to be Catholic. There exists a prevailing *negative attitude* to past Catholicism. Even Pope John Paul II (in 1995 and 1996) apologized--not for his own errors and failings--but for the imagined failings and sins of the *past* Church, Christ's Roman Catholic Church.

It's *in* to speak negatively about Traditional Catholicism. New Age Catholics lead the way in criticizing faithful Catholics. "*Tua* culpa" has become an invective which is hurled at the past. Instead, their "*tua culpa*" should be replaced with a humble and sincere "*mea* culpa." By the way, who ever heard of a confessional "*tua culpa?*"

New Age Catholicism has made Catholics in the USA into good citizens of the USSA. Many bishops have betrayed God and thus betrayed mankind. They have wounded or even destroyed institutional Catholicism--by what they did and by what they failed to do. Thus, have they wounded or destroyed decent God-based state-government by what they have done and have failed to do.

This reminds me of Padre Pio's comment on the Third Secret of Fatima. *"Beware of the bishops!"* he said. Are we not also to pray and sacrifice for the Bishop of Rome--as we hear his words, and deeds reported in the secular press? He declared that *"Evolution is more than an hypothesis."* Despite his own acknowledgment that (according to the scientific method) *"a theory proves its validity to the degree that it submits to verification,"* as any honest scientist will assure you--*there exists no verification for evolution.* (Times Picayune, Nov. 12, 1996; Clarion Herald, Catholic News Service, Nov. 14, 1996)

Evolution, as commonly perceived, is totally antithetical to believing in *God as revealed,* and is the foundation of Russia's Error. Such an espousal of evolution is the renunciation of classical Christianity, (both Catholic and non-Catholic). It is a changing of loyalties from God to man. It is the heart of Chardin's theological philosophy, which was officially and bindingly condemned by the Church for all times and places. In effect, for the ordinary person, his loyalty or allegiance is manipulatively being changed from *God as revealed* to man as deceiving and as deceived. Deception is perceived as truth by "good-willed" older people, and accepted as Bible truth by the rest of the people. Only the remnant few see through the deception--

that is, how and why the above statement is true. All is consistent with Beria's disclosure in 1932.

The changing of loyalty consists, in its primary step, of the eradication of existing loyalties. This can be done in one of two ways. First, by demonstrating that previously existing loyalties have brought about intellectual embarrassment, perilous physical circumstances, such as imprisonment, lack of recognition, duress or privation, and second, by eradication of the personality itself. (Beria's talk, 16)

Relative to our example, has not belief in creation been propagandized as being intellectually embarrassing? On a wider scale, evil churchmen teach that loyalty to traditional Catholicism produces horrible results. To eradicate the personality, in the primary or soft stage, they make fun of (or instill hatred against) those who dare to uphold what they proclaim to be *the outdated past* and who dare to go against the politically correct--politely, positively, presently and pleasantly correct. Ultimately, they force their victims to denounce and abandon *God as revealed* and to be subject to them--pawns of Satan.

As Beria pronounced, psychopolitical leaders must go about *"defaming or degrading the individual whose loyalties are to be changed.* " (Beria's talk, 17) Isn't this exactly what modern Russia has accomplished? Modern Russia has reduced human beings not only to animals, but to demoralized or "broken" animals, who prefer the state-provided zoo to God-given freedom.

Sounds like the average chancery policy to its priests, doesn't it? Indeed, New Age Catholicism employs this same satanic methodology within its priest-culture. I remember in the sixties their treatment of a priest who wouldn't abandon the Canonized (Tridentine) Liturgy. How dare he not abandon and renounce the Apostolic Liturgy, the Mass as instituted by Christ, at the command of the bishops or of superiors?

For example, Beria's tactics were employed on Fr. Schell, S.J. We were told that he was "a mental case." Why? He wouldn't discard that which was declared to be outmoded--the traditional or canonized Mass and classical or binding Catholicism. As the years have proved--Fr. Schell was not only sane, but also saintly.

Eventually--as with New Age Catholicism--the cooperative victims of evil propaganda are led to believe the absurd. I will cite only a few examples: that *multis* means *all* and no longer means *many;* that the early church devoutly practiced sacrilege (communion) in the hand; and that divorce annulment-style isn't really divorce.

After the population abandons truth for the politically correct, then the population is reduced to being a herd of animal-men, which must be zooed. Satan rewards the zoo-keepers with extra goodies. Satan rewards the zooed with security. The state and the *state-defined* or *community-defined* existential church become like unto a god which cares for and nurtures. There is no other god but reigning experts and authorities and their enforcers. The zooed humans are controlled by the authorities through fear and force.

However, it's still a God-designed world. As it were, God will inevitably "bleed through" the world as "re-created" by man. The wages of sin are death and destruction--even in this world. For example, in the gem of the zooed nations--Russia from the fifties to the nineties--conditions for the *zooed animal men* became so oppressive that by way of a few examples: one had to wait in lines forty to fifty hours a week to get a minimum amount of toilet paper and cabbage for himself and his family; most married women were driven to have an average of four abortions; one-fourth of the zooed were tortured; there were only two or three needles per hospital for necessary injections.

Russia's Error--the abandonment of God--brings about the degradation of men both in time and eternity. This is Satan's hour. Recognize it so you can respond to reality intelligently. Recognize that we are under Fatima's Curse, so that you may be inspired to pray and sacrifice the pope into activating the God-given Fatima Opportunity and so that you may take proper action to save yourself and yours in these evil times.

IV. Aggravate the masses into seeking our Utopia. Then deliver them into evil. Promise Utopia. Deliver *Hell on earth*.

First of all, make the masses seek freedom from the only entity that could fulfill them--the Catholic Church. Image or project the Church as the evil from which one must seek to be delivered. Promise the people *freedom from religion*, even as you deliver them into the hands of narrow-minded, God-rejecting, hateful tyrants, whose only god is man and thus, Satan.

> The psychopolitical operative, in his program of degradation, should at all times bring into question any family that is deeply religious, and, should any neurosis or insanity be occasioned in that family, he should blame and hold responsible their religious connections for the neurotic or psychotic condition. Religion must be made synonymous with neurosis and psychosis. People who are deeply religious should be held to be less and less responsible for their own sanity and should more and more be given over to the ministrations of psychopolitical operatives. (Beria's talk, 42)

Those psychopolitical operatives predicated by Beria in 1932 now abound. Russia's Error is now more successful in New Age Catholicism and the USA than in the USSR. Within the church, I am led to recall and pray for the vast multitude of traditionalist priests who were sentenced by their bishops to psychological manipulation, or who were persecuted and even dismissed.

Does not the first part of this Beria-quote remind you of the Waco murders--1993? These people were murdered for being religious. Yet, the American bishops and the populace were not disturbed by this.

My prediction is that we'll see more "Wacos" in the coming years of our rapid descent into Russia's Error and the New Order.

Aggravate one race against another, the privileged abnormals against the normals and the poor against the rich. Collapse will come. Then, come in as saviors. That's Satan's plan.

Aggravate or cause unrest. For example, reward premarital sex with abortion or free support for the baby. For example, blame the rich for burdening the masses. Tax the rich. Punish them. Punish anyone who dares to develop or use his talents and get rich in the process of doing so. Create *government subsidized privileged classes* such as: teen mothers, homosexuals and welfare clients. Such creations must bring about chaos, which will then require the state's intervention.

Aggravate. Sooner or later a break-down will occur. Then, come in promising Utopia--by imposing order on an unbearable chaos. Remember that these plans which are materializing in our apocalyptic *now* were devised by Satan-inspired Beria in 1932 as disclosed previously and as illustrated below.

The handling of economic propaganda is not properly the sphere of psychopolitics but the psychopolitician must understand economic measures and the Communist goals connected with them.

The masses must at last come to believe that only excessive taxation of the rich can relieve them of the 'burdensome leisure class' and can thus be brought to accept such a thing as an income tax, a Marxist principle smoothly slid into the Capitalistic framework in 1909 in the United States. This, even though the basic law of the United States forbade it, and even though communism at that time had been active only a few years in America. So successful was the income tax law, that had it been followed thoroughly, it could have brought the United States and not Russia into the world scene as the first Communist nation. (Beria's talk, 47).

That's quite a statement. However, do you realize we live in a republic, a constitutional republic? This republic was *violated,* by imposing income tax-- according to the Russian Error expert, Beria.

What are the duties of the state? Are they not very limited--to providing and upkeeping roads; to maintaining an army and a very few other specified duties. By creating and fulfilling new needs, the state is led to impose greater and greater taxation, which is equivalent to robbing the decent in order to support, enrich and promote *privileged* classes, which live from *entitlement programs.*

"This nation will be great until it votes benefits for its people out of the public treasury"--de Tocqueville concerning the USA. Now, we have voted multiplied benefits for certain privileged groups or classes of people out of our non-existent public treasury. We have not voted for benefits and paid for them out of the Public Treasury. We have gone in debt, so that politicians may win votes as this nation descends into Socialist dictatorship. Certainly the ever-worsening financial crisis will blow up in our faces. Then, chaos will reign and the state will come to us as savior--since, by then, we will have no other savior, king or lord, but Caesar (Jn 19:15).

However, in these circumstances the state will save us by enslaving us--by bringing us into servitude to the USSA and then to Russia. I believe you can see why Beria's insight is not only true for us but is also *more than true.* Beria's insights explain the Fatima Curse--that Russia's Errors will invade the world and that Russia will be used by God to punish mankind for its awesome sinfulness.

We are now going the same route that other socialist dictatorships have gone--dictatorships such as Nazi Germany, Fascist Italy, Communist Russia and Communist China. Russia's Error in the form of Socialism invaded the world from 1917 to 1989. Russia's Error as the New World Order is now invading the world--especially, the USA.

> Russia's Error will spread throughout the world. Nations will be annihilated. Russia will be used as My instrument for destruction--God, describing the Fatima Curse.

Remember what is leading us into chaos--the *sin of love*. This sin enthrones man as it dethrones God and His revealed Will. We are immersed in the diabolically feminine--we love *man*, not God. What demonic madness! No wonder Our Lady of Fatima has disclosed that she "finds it difficult" to prevent God's wrath from saturating mankind.

PAUSE FOR SANITY

Many New Age Catholics are shocked by my sentiments. They have become indoctrinated into accepting the mega-sin of socialism or of "Love, American Church Style." Such blinded people have imaged and bowed before the "God of love." To such blinded people, it seems natural for the State (perceived as the "God of Love's agent") to be positive and loving to man as he is, especially, as sinful. This state loves. It must be charitable.

The state as *being charitable* is a meaningless phrase in itself. *Charity* is defined as being between individuals--not between the Sovereign State and its subjects. Socialism destroys *God as revealed* to create a false god--the god of love.

Justice is not primarily to be defined by man. God is in charge. God is to be legislator of our justice--our proper and due relationship to Him and to our fellow man. Justice is our Father's Will being fulfilled--*God's Will as revealed* being done on earth, according to His Heavenly Pattern, as revealed to us in the Bible and in His Church. Primarily, justice is to be directed to God. God is to be adored and obeyed as He has commanded (in His Revelations).

Thus, the Catholic Church is to be the only religion for whole communities--within which, adults and families are free to join or not, as long as they don't establish another church, or in any other way impose error or sin upon others. Why? Error has no rights.

All of this is Catholic Dogma as explained by Pope Leo XIII, Pope Saint Pius X, Pope Pius XI, Pope Pius XII and others. God is to be enthroned. Man is to obey *God as revealed,* not be as a god.

Justice of man towards man should be legislated and enforced *in the light of authentic Catholic teachings* by the state which would have, for the most part, a minimal police role. In a Catholic USA, we would not have two million people in the criminal class as we do today. A Catholic USA would not suffer nearly four million violent crimes each year, as we now do. A Catholic USA would not be socialist--a victim and victimizer of Russia's Error.

Look back at the imperfect--yet, going in the right direction--Catholic Dark and Middle Ages. One out of five adults lived in the service of God as well as *in service to others* for the love of God. One out of five adults was a dedicated celibate. God first--then, men are happy. Men first--then Satan dominates.

The traditional Catholic Church is totally antithetic to new age Catholicism--to Catholicism as imaged and imposed by reigning experts and authorities. Let's reflect on a typical quote from *authentic and binding* Catholic teachings--as written in a binding encyclical. (Those after 1958 aren't *binding* encyclicals, according to the expressed intentions of the popes who wrote them.)

Man's natural right of possessing and transmitting property by inheritance must remain intact and cannot be taken away by the State from man. For man precedes the State and the domestic household, is antecedent, as well in idea as in fact, to the gathering of men into a community. [Rerum Novarum, Pope Leo XIII, par. 6, 1891]

The right to possess private property is derived from nature, not from man; and the State has by no means the right to abolish it. [Rerum Novarum, Pope Leo XIII, par. 121]

BACK TO SATAN'S PLANS FOR OUR PRESENT AND OUR FUTURE

If all goes as it is going, then eventually and inevitably, Russia will conquer--by force or by threat of force--when (not if) the American economy "bellies up," or some other crisis develops. Then, we will be at Russia's mercy. Then we will be enslaved to Russian perverts--as Beria himself predicted way back in 1932.

By perverting the institutions of a nation and bringing about a general degradation, by interfering with the economics of a nation to the degree that privation and depression become commonplace, only minor shocks will be necessary to produce, on the populace as a whole, an obedient reaction. Thus, the mere threat of war, the mere threat of bombings, could cause the population to sue instantly for peace. It is a long and arduous road for the psychopolitical operative to achieve this state of mind on the part of a whole nation, but no more than twenty or thirty years should be necessary to run the entire program. Having at hand, as we do, weapons with which to accomplish the goal. (Beria's talk, 48)

Beria's prediction of thirty years was a bit too optimistic but how could he figure on World War II--Hitler's embracing Russia's Error--delaying Russia's program? In any case, it's of little consolation to us or to our children that Beria's predictions will come true much later than he predicted--in our, or our children's, lifetime.

V. RULE BY DEMONIC DECEPTION, FEAR AND SUB-SAVAGE FORCE.

Do you remember the five-year plans--the carrots, which were presented to control the Russian masses up to 1990 or so? Sedate the masses. Promise them anything. Get them to live for utopia on earth. Then, they will reject Catholicism.

That reminds me of the present existential church. We work for Evangelism 2000, even as the upper clergy deliver us over to Satan. It is rather paradoxical and *poetically just* that, according to reliable archaeologists, this very Fatima Conference[2] most likely occurs in the two thousandth year since

---

2

Referring to the Fatima Congress on World Peace and the Immaculate Heart of Mary held in Rome on November 18-23, 1996. This book is an enhanced text of Fr. Trinchard's talk to the bishops at this Congress.

the birth of Christ.

1996 is Christ-oriented. In contrast, 2000 is man-oriented. In 2000, man hopes to unite religiously, much as men once strove to religiously unite in the creation of the Tower of Babel. Also, it is rather paradoxical and poetically just that (according to archaeological evidence), the meeting place of the world religions in 2000 A.D., *will not be the real Mount Sinai upon which Moses received the Ten Commandments.*

The magic year of 2000 could be the mega-tragic year of 2000. Read God's writing on the wall: Your deeds have been judged and found wanting. Therefore, your New World Order will be taken away from you--*mene tekel; peres* (Dn 5:25).

> The Capitalist does not know the definition of war. He thinks of war as attack with force performed by soldiers and machines. He does not know that a more effective if somewhat longer war can be fought with bread or, in our case, with drugs and the wisdom of our art. In truth, the Capitalist has never won a war. The psychopolitician is having little trouble winning this one. (Beria's talk, 14).

Russia and its Error are conquering the world, as

predicted by God at Fatima, as it were, not by physical force, but by spiritual and psychological force. Russia and Russia's Error have been increasingly successful in conquering the world since 1917, exactly as predicted by Fatima--and will continue to do so, as Beria advises us. Until the Church is repared and its pope activates the Fatima Opportunity, Russia will be used by God to punish the world and "Russia's Error will spread throughout the world."

CONTROLLING ANIMALS

In the following text, note that the code word *hypnotism* means *the adoration of,* and *full obedience to* man--as defined and imposed by reigning experts and authority. Other key words such as *unconsciousness* and *animal* correctly refer to the victims of Russia's Error. As fallen from God, they are referred to as degenerates, or as animals.

If you would have obedience you must have no compromise with humanity. If you would have obedience you must make it clearly understood that you have no mercy. Man is an animal. He understands, in the final analysis, only those things that a brute understands.

As an example of this, we find an individual refusing to obey and being struck. His refusal to obey is now less vociferous. He is struck again, and his resistance is lessened once more. He is hammered and pounded again and again, until, at length, his only thought is direct and implicit obedience to that person from whom the force has come. This is a proven principle. It is proven because it is the main principle that Man, the animal, has used since his earliest beginnings. It is the only principle that has been effective, the only principle that has brought about a wide and continued belief. For it is to our benefit that an individual who is struck again, and again, and again from a certain source, will, at length, hypnotically believe anything he is told by the wielder of the blows.

The stupidity of Western civilizations is best demonstrated by the fact that they believe hypnotism is a thing of the mind, of attention, and a desire for unconsciousness. This is not true. Only when a person has been beaten, punished, and mercilessly hammered, can hypnotism upon him be guaranteed to be effective. It is stated by Western authorities on hypnosis that only some twenty percent of the people are susceptible to hypnotism. This statement is untrue. Given enough punishment, all people in any time and place are susceptible to hypnotism. In other words, the addition of force makes hypnotism uniformly effective.

Where unconsciousness could not be induced by simple concentration upon the hypnotist, unconsciousness can be induced by drugs, by blows, by electric shock, and by other means. And where unconsciousness cannot be induced so as to make an implantation or an hypnotic command effective, it is only necessary to amputate the functioning portions of the animal man's brain to render him null and void and no longer a menace. Thus, we find that hypnotism is entirely effective.

The mechanisms of hypnotism demonstrate clearly that people can be made to believe in certain conditions, and even in their environment or in politics, by the administration of force. Thus, it is necessary for a psychopolitician to be an expert in the administration of force. Thus, he can bring about implicit obedience, not only on the part of individual members of the populace, but on the entire populace itself and its government. He need only take unto himself a sufficiently savage role, a sufficiently uncompromising inhuman attitude, and he will be obeyed and believed. (Beria's talk 24, 25)

Here you have it. Socialism must rule by fear and force. Satan rules on earth as he does in Hell. Hate and inhuman cruelty are sub-savagely inflicted on the victims of Russia's Error--the rejection and dethronement of God and the enthronement of man and thus, of Satan. Most comply. A few go insane. Very few refuse to succumb to Russia's Error. These love God totally and exclusively. They conquer even when conquered. (Heb 11 and Apoc 12)

Either men will be ruled by God or they will be sub-savagely tyrannized by man and thus, by Satan. Those who live according to principles will not live for pleasure or popularity or out of fear of Godless force. It is impossible to subject a true Catholic (as described in the twelfth chapter of the Apocalypse) to the New World Order or to the *new and improved version* of Russia's Error. Think about this!

Lest you are tempted to think that the man-originating New World Order will be too nice to be cruel, I close this chapter with a subsequent quote from Beria which is totally substantiated by Russia's and China's cruel and inhuman murdering of well over 200 million of their own people. Know your enemy. Try to visualize what he will do to you and yours when he comes into America.

> Obedience is the result of force...The most barbaric, unrestrained, brutal use of force, if carried far enough, invokes obedience. Savage force, sufficiently long deployed against any individual, will bring about his concurrence with any principle or order.
>
> Force is the antithesis of humanizing action. It is so synonymous in the human mind with savagery, lawlessness, brutality, and barbarism, that it is only necessary to display an inhuman attitude toward people, to be granted by those people control over them.
>
> Any organization that has the spirit and courage to display inhumanity, savagery, brutality, and an uncompromising lack of humanity, will be obeyed. Such a use of force is, itself, the essential ingredient of greatness. (Beria's talk, 27).

New Age Catholicism, the USSA, Nazi Germany, Russia, etc. rule by fear and force--exactly as planned. Why? Russia's Error (as Communism or the New World Order) dethroned God and enthrones natural man! Natural man is naturally satanic.

Russia hasn't disowned the use of force in the past fifty years. It has only refined and perfected its sub-savage inhumanity to man. Satan comes to destroy and to kill--not to give life or a better quality of life.

Either way--by inducing, frighteningly or forcefully, obedience to them or by most cruelly murdering--perverted proponents of Russia's Error win in this world. Satan wins. Only Mary's Remnant conquer even as they are conquered (cf. Rv 12).

VI.   GRADUALLY REPLACE THE TRUE CHURCH WITH A FALSE ONE.

Get the existential church to betray Christ, and to become the Second Beast--at least, in spirit, if not also in fact. I must admit that I am inserting this step *into* Beria's talk. However, it is clearly contained within the important "Li Wei Han" document issued from Communist China (1959) as the directive to be used in converting Cuba.

This document was inspired by the success of Stalin in making the superficially religious Russian

Orthodox Schismatic Church into the Russian Church and thereby a puppet of satanic socialism. This document tells us how the New World Order will convert religions into being consonant with the spirit of the Second Beast.

These satanic ecclesial conversion techniques are very important since they've been used to create and nourish New Age Catholicism since 1960. New Age Catholicism isn't traditional Catholicism. However, only the truly *faith-filled* can perceive this negative truth.

New Age Catholicism will continue to thrive within the existential church, until the pope activates the Fatima Opportunity. The existential church-- especially in the USA--is no longer Catholic as even a famous curial cardinal was forced to admit. *"The Church in America is in schism"*--Cardinal Gagnon. This church is in schism in as much as it is *in heresy.*

The satanic plan to destroy and to subvert the existential church have been given to us or are implied in the two official directives which were (and still are) used as blueprints to implement or execute Satan's will for the existential church of Christ. Such a will has been (increasingly) executed by evil Judas-bishops within the Church. Be as wise as these serpents. At least, be able to identify them, from inspecting their fruits and perceiving that their fruits are bad or evil.

RUSSIA'S ERROR APPLIED TO THE CHURCHES
AS DISCLOSED IN CHINA--1959

God, Satan and the truly informed know that (as the Fatima Message states) as the existential church goes so go nations, and so goes the world. Therefore, the proponents of Russia's Errors must focus on the existential Catholic Church--to make it evil and to make it ever more evil. The Two Beasts work hand in hand for our defeat. (Apoc. 13)

Before I proceed, I'm led to pause in order to clear up what might be bothering you. *"He's supposed to be considering Russia's Error, yet he keeps coming back to the existential church. Why?"*

As the Fatima Message assures us, we are in a crucial spiritual battle. So far, Satan is winning the battle. So far, we are under the Fatima Curse. De facto, the existential church is now becoming increasingly unfaithful to God. This church is now becoming ever more cursed by God. Therefore, we all live under God's ever worsening, end-times curse--the Fatima Curse.

Satanic communist forces have placed within the

Catholic Church establishment, an influential group of bishops and priests. These now implement Satan's plan for the Church.

As part of the program to destroy religion from within, in the late 1950's the KGB started sending dedicated young Communists to ecclesiastical academies and seminaries to train them as future Church leaders. These young Communists joined the Church, *not at the call of their consciences to serve God,* but at the call of the Communist Party in order to serve that Party and to implement its general line in the struggle against religion...In the present phase secret agents in the Catholic Churches...implement Communist strategy.(The Perestroika Deception, Anatoliy Golitsyn, London/New York: Edward Harle Ltd., 1995, italics mine)

As of 1997, these *"secret agents in the Catholic Churches"* refer to the KGB-assigned seminarians, who are now influential priests and bishops as revealed by Bella Dodd, Golitsyn and others. These are Satan's ecclesial agents who apply Russia's Error to the ecclesial establishment.

At least, by God's graces, let's acknowledge reality. Only then can we properly and gracefully respond. Now, let's consider a six-fold--A-B-C-D-E-F--

Satanic Plan to undermine and pervert Catholicism. Remember, Satan, the most wise liar--the father of lies, now deems it profitable to keep the appearance of church, while destroying its *true essence*.

A. KEEP THE APPEARANCE OF CATHOLICISM WHILE CHANGING ITS ESSENCE.

Why *Catholicism*? As God, the informed few and Satan know--Catholicism is the one and only true religion. It alone fulfills each man's innate burden or purpose--to know, love and serve God as God commands and thus to be happy now and forever. Through Catholicism--especially canonized Masses--comes the major anti-satanic power or force.

The Li Wei Han document (printed in the People's Republic of China) explicitly discloses Russia's erroneous plan--*"to progressively replace religious elements by the Marxist element...to lead Catholics to destroy themselves and the divine."* (Li Wei Han Document)

Let's see how this simple plan is being accomplished. *"The objective to be attained, what we are fighting for, is to destroy the Church."* (Li Wei Han Document) Remember, it is the true or Traditional

Church that is to be destroyed--not its counterfeit.

B. Impose Russia's Error. Steadily replace God-centeredness with man-centeredness.

As you read the following, note the code-words. For example, *political consciousness* means *living for/from this world or for/from man, and not God. Marxist element* simply stated is *Russia's Error.*

The line of action to be followed against the Church consists in instructing, educating, persuading, convincing, and gradually awakening and fully developing the political consciousness of Catholics through obtaining their participation in study groups and political activities. We must undertake [engage in] the dialectical struggle within religion through the instrumentality of activists (militant agents within the Church). We will progressively replace the religious element by the Marxist element, gradually change the false consciousness into a true consciousness, so that Catholics will eventually destroy of their own accord and on their own account, the divine images...That is our line of action in the struggle for victory against the counter-revolutionary Catholic Church. (Li Wei Han Document, p. 27)

Political consciousness is the sin of love promulgated and implemented in its various forms. *Political consciousness* defines the American Church. For example, the heresy of Americanism (see the encyclical on Americanism by Pope Leo XII), leads contemporary American "Catholics" to do anything in order to be accepted by non-Catholics, *anything*, especially, to betray the Catholic Dogma that *extra ecclesiam, nulla salus*-- outside of the Church, there is no salvation.

To a greater extent than you realize, the American Church has destroyed Catholicism while keeping an appearance of being Catholic. It has earned an "A" in implementing the <u>Li Wei Han Document</u>.

American Catholics love man, not God. American upper clergy lead the way. They'll give up any God-revelation that gets in the way of their love of man (community or individuals) with the notable exception of Catholic traditionalists, of course.

"Catholics will eventually destroy of their own accord and on their own account, the divine images." While this concretely reminds us of so many contemporary churches--stripped and devoid of divine images as are Protestant halls--does this not

concretely demonstrate that not only church decor, but the very image of *God Himself as revealed* has been destroyed by "Catholics" themselves?

C. Replace adoration of, allegiance to and obedience to God with any politically correct God-rejecting, psychological, man-created theory or philosophy.

Each of us is made to know, love and obey *God as He revealed Himself to us,* and as He commands us through His Revelations. Russia's Error replaces God with man, and, *as He commands through His Revelations,* with *as reigning experts and authorities command through their edicts.*

You must know that until recent times the entire subject of mental derangement, whether so light as simple worry or so heavy as insanity, was the sphere of activity of the church and only the church. Traditionally, both in civilized and barbaric nations, the priesthood alone had complete charge of the mental condition of the citizen.

We must insist that *scientific practices* be applied to the problem of the mind. Without this official insistence or even if it were to be relaxed for a moment, the masses would reach out for the priest...whenever mental conditions came into question. Today, in Europe and America, scientific practices in the field of the mind would not last moments, if not routinely enforced by officialdom.

Care must be taken to hide the fact that the incidence of insanity has increased only since these scientific practices started to be applied. (Beria, 59)

Recently, certain schools of psychology and of counseling have come to realize and acknowledge the primary place of religion in our lives. True religion produces healthy minds. True religion, not any man-made psychology, is of greatest health value, as well as of primary importance. In spite of this, within the establishment, most bishops, priests and counselors enthrone psychology and dethrone religion--as preferred theology and therapy.

D. Gradually, but *effectively*, subject the Church to the State--or to reigning experts and authorities.

This process is implemented differently in the USA than called for in the China directive. The end result is the same. Get the Church to follow, or at least *not impede*, the State--the will of the people, as defined by reigning experts and authorities.

Furthermore, we will present a program of tactics applied with success in the Chinese People's Republic in order to liberate the Chinese people from the influence of the Imperialist Catholic Church of Rome.

The Church and its faithful must be induced to take part in the People's government so that the masses may exert their influence on them. The Church cannot be permitted to preserve its character which places it above the will of the masses. (Li Wei Han Document, p. 28)

The goal is to direct the existential church away from *God as revealed* and to man. *The goal* is *to bring about an existential church divorced from the Church.* Indeed, in many places, the existential church is already divorced from the faith and morals (morals as social and liturgical) of the--*semper et ubique idem*--the *in all times and places the same*-- Catholic Church.

This document could not have foreseen the success of the evil Spirit of Vatican II (Russia's Error abiding within the existential church) in metamorphasizing the Church from within. Is not the present pope/Rome axis out of line with the perennial or Roman Catholic See as it existed *semper et ubique idem* before 1960? Until this question is answered dogmatically, each is not only free, but obliged to answer this question as thoroughly and as best he can.

Do not the wishes of each bishop or each national or world group of bishops since 1960 allegedly define the will of the *people* or the will of the *people's government*? *WE are church* ultimately means that the Church is *as instituted by "ever-improving" man and not as instituted by Christ.* In fact, does not the following directive describe the present diplomacy or tactics of pope/Rome as it staggers back and forth apparently standing for orthodoxy, yet favoring Russia's Error?

> If the bonds between the masses and the Church are very close, the principle of two steps forward and one step backward should be followed. In taking the step backward the People's government must state that it is defending religious freedom and that by the will of the masses, it is establishing reform committees in the associations so that the

patriotic masses may express themselves more directly in the leadership of the affairs of the Church. (Li Wei Han Document, p. 28)

E. Create issues. Focus on certain issues.

Create, properly phrase and sloganize issues Sloganize solutions. Impose these as the will of the people. Flush out and eliminate dissidents. "Guns kill...We need Health Care...Cigarettes are unhealthy ...We must care for the poor...We must legislate and implement Children's Rights...Do not homosexuals have a right to marry?...Is there not a right to die?"

Sloganize! Recently, the news depicted a Halloween haunted house designed by *fundamentalists*. Within this house sinners were depicted and their eternal fate disclosed. The "American public"--as created by Russia's Error--objected. Why? These shows were discriminatory! True--but that's the way God is and will be on judgment day and eternally. No matter how much Americans may object--God discriminates!

Slogans, slogans, slogans! "Dialogue and change"-- when the liberals are trying to attain power. "Conform or else"--after they attain power. "We have a right to participate in the liturgy...Caring is granting annulments...Caring is understanding how hard or impossible it is not to contracept... Priests must face the people in saying Mass...The people are entitled to commit 'sacrilege in the hand'...etc."

> Slogans must be followed. It is patriotic to adhere to the government and to observe the laws...Disobedience is unpatriotic...The associations must profess their patriotism...The unpatriotic elements must be eliminated from the associations and judged as criminals by the masses...It is the duty of every citizen to punish these criminals...The militants must turn the masses against these criminal elements...As soon as the masses have eliminated these criminals from the community, they must be judged under the provisions of the laws of the People's government. (Li Wei Han Document, p. 29)

Once evil forces control any establishment, they ruthlessly flush out criminals or dissidents. Certainly, the American Church does this remarkably well, especially, within the ranks of its clergy, its seminarians and lay bureaucrats. Do all of this in the name of unity and peace and out of the love of man as an individual or as community--love, love, love, never obedience to *God as revealed* out of love or fear of Him.

Within the societal government of the USA, we are on the verge of going into a diabolically masculine stage. In this stage, non-productive members of the community--such as old people, welfare clients and sexual perverts--will soon be treated as criminals destined for murder by the state. Within the church, non-conforming or traditionalist Catholics will increasingly be treated as outcasts. Already, such troublemakers are the only ones condemned to Hell by liberal pastors across the land.

> The People's government must push in depth [to the utmost] the discussion of all disagreements. During these discussions, care should be taken to discover the counter-revolutionists who had previously gone unnoticed. (Li Wei Han Document, p. 29).

Flush out the trouble-makers. Then flush thcm away. Get rid of them. The *man-community* must function smoothly.

F. Liturgize Russia's Error. "Lex orandi, lex credendi." Make sure the people *pray Russia's Error*, so that they may come to fully believe Russia's Error.

I didn't make this up! It's in the <u>Li Wei Han</u> <u>Document</u>. Evil liturgical implementation in the name of a deliberately falsified Vatican Two was predicted by the Communists. This liturgical revolution was executed exactly as described by Chinese Communists. In the Novus Ordo (New Order) English Liturgy, Russia's Error is boldly prayed. Therefore, the *Catholic masses in the USA* come to strongly believe in Russia's Error. Let's see how the <u>Li Wei Han Document</u> teaches this.

> Once the key posts of the clergy are in our hands and submitted to the People's Government, one will proceed to progressively eliminating from the liturgy those elements which are incompatible with the People's Government. The first changes will affect the Mass, sacraments and other devotions. Then, the masses will be protected against all pressure and all obligation to put in an appearance in church. (<u>Li Wei Han Document</u>, p. 30)

Indeed, the Novus Ordo English (versions of the) Liturgy has surpassed China's expectations. They constitute a positive expression of Russia's Error. Indeed, rumors about the *Masonic spirit* controlling very much of the uppermost church seem to be true. There is now little substantial difference between Masonic Liturgy and modern *Catholic liturgies as enacted* in the USA. This last part of our quote exposes both the Novus Ordo English Liturgy as it exists in the USA and its creators and implementors for what they are--*destroyers*. Ultimately, they are putting even themselves out of business--just as planned and predicted by the <u>Li Wei Han Document</u>.

Who wants to bother to *liturgize man-worship*? Why bother? Why not worship *yourself--man*--by playing golf or sleeping? *De facto*, Mass attendance is now less than one-fourth of what it was before the revolting sixties.

Understand your enemy. See the *extent* of his successes. Only then can you be certainly motivated to fight the enemy. Only then will you believe and implement as best you can God's Fatima solution-- the Fatima Opportunity--the opportunity to change this awesome curse into an awesome blessing.

Know the elementary methodology successfully employed by Satan to bring about his kingdom on earth in our times. Become familiar with the characteristics of the Two Beasts of the Apocalypse (Ch 13) and the four methodologies employed as the end-times vehicle which embodies and promulgates Russia's Error.

SATAN'S SPECIAL ECCLESIAL TACTICS

Satan's primary concern is perverting the existential church. Having greatly succeeded in doing so--as predicted and as honestly verifiable from the many crises areas which worsen day by day--Satan now uses existential churches which are impregnated with New Age Catholicism as his primary agents for spreading Russia's Error.

New Age Catholicism is like unto the Second Beast of the Apocalypse. This Beast merges with nations who are embracing (or who have embraced) Russia's Error, which are like unto the First Beast of the Apocalypse (Ch. 13). The soul (or live force) of this merger, (union or marriage) is the soul of Satan.

Life is *awesomely dangerous today*. This is the *worst of times*. We are in times devoid of positive God-directed Catholic devotion or devoid of what Fr. Malachi Martin so aptly describes as Catholic *intimacy with the Divine*.

Much of what you've read in Beria's talk and in the Li Wei Han Document applies to some existential "Catholic" churches. These churches willingly embrace and implement the *spirit* of the Novus Ordo Seclorum--the New World Order--Russia's Error.

METHODOLOGY

Certain processes can be perceived which are used in the American church to form disciples for the Second Beast--in spirit, if not also in fact. Remember, the goal of New Age Catholicism and Russia's Error in the New Order is the same goal as the Fatima-defined Russia's Error--to dethrone God and enthrone man.

I. TRUTH CAN NO LONGER BE FOUND IN THE PAST

Satan uses a type of jujitsu on his ecclesial victims. He takes away their support from the *past which defined and defines what a Catholic must be and do.* Then, through reigning ecclesial ' experts and authorities, he extends a hand of support. However, such support is provided by lies or by that which is useless toward salvation. Such apparent support works against the victim. When people have become convinced that they can't find the truth in the past, how can they find the truth? They can't rely on classical tradition--especially, Apostolic Tradition. They can't rely on books from the past, especially, the Bible.

Victims of New Age Catholicism *can't* find truth *as revealed by God or His true Church.* Even presently approved Bible *versions* must be politically correct and *not traditional.* Why do I state *versions?* No longer do reigning experts claim to give us *translations* of the Bible. At least, they are honest in their deception.

Victims of New Age Catholicism have been indoctrinated about the liturgical past. In the past, we are deceptively assured, there were *many* vastly different canons or Mass prayers. Therefore, one can't claim that any Mass prayers come from Christ. Therefore, the Mass wasn't instituted by Christ. That's all He did was express a desire that we perform some sort of memorial service of His life and death, preferably a meal and not a sacrifice.

Truth from the past--especially as contained in Apostolic Tradition--can no longer be discovered.

Experts assure us that ancient documents are unreliable, false or outdated. Confusion and darkness reign supreme. Satan's kingdom has taken over within many existential churches.

II. REIGNING EXPERTS AND AUTHORITIES TELL YOU WHAT IS CORRECT. ONE MUST SUBMIT HIS CONSCIENCE TO REIGNING EXPERTS AND AUTHORITIES.

In many existential churches--in those churches which embrace and impose New Age Catholicism-- one can't believe in Catholic teachings as being *idem*--the same--or *semper*--always true. In such churches, one must exchange his God-orientation for man-orientation. One must submit his conscience to present-day reigning experts and authorities. They will guide us. In the diabolically masculine modality of Russia's Error, the reigning experts and authorities propagandize and demand conformity to the presently, positively, episcopally and *politically correct*.

Sound familiar? These are classical Communist tactics. The State and/or the politically correct existential churches will be your shepherds. They, not Christ, are the truth, the way and the life. The State and the political (New Age) church--through reigning experts and authorities--will direct us into political correctness, which replaces truth, especially, God-given truth.

For example, in the USA in many places, we have evolved American Masses. Attending one of these "Masses" is like attending a *high church protestant service,* at best; and a New World Order (Novus Ordo Seclorum) liturgy, at worst. As we have seen, liberal churches tend to be far more dictatorial than conservative ones. Rule under any man--lay or clerical--who has dethroned *God as revealed* is subjection to the very worst tyranny.

III. NEW AGE CATHOLICISM AND REIGNING EXPERTS IN THE NEW ORDER GIVE THE FIRST DIRECTIVE: THE DIABOLICALLY FEMININE MODALITY.

To fit into the New Age religion, New Age Catholicism, in effect, insists that Catholicism has been replaced by a new religion. In this new religion, Original Sin, real personal sins, eternal Hell and other unpleasantries have been outlawed. This is New Age Catholicism in its diabolically feminine modality. There is no Sin. There is no real Hell. All are saved. Each man's life is *no fault*. Each is free to define *"God"* to his own image and liking.

As diabolically feminine, New Age Catholicism assures us that there is no such thing as a Hell-deserving sin. There is no real *sin*, no real *Hell* and your life is *no fault* (as even the English version of the <u>Catechism of the Catholic Church</u> of 1992 reiterated). Why? God is too good to send anyone to Hell. God is so good that *He lets you define Him into existence, as He is created to your own image, as you like Him to be.*

All are saved since Christ somehow dwells in each of us. Hell, as a real place in time and eternity, evaporates since, as we are assured in the new Catechism, man could only go there if he *auto-excluded* himself from Heaven (according to the English version of the <u>Catechism of the Catholic Church</u> of 1992). New Age Catholicism assures us that there's no longer a Hell to fear and thus, no *one and only religion given by God* necessary for salvation from Hell. New Age Catholicism brings about the self-destruction of the Church--*self-destruction, as confessed even by Pope Paul VI.*

Let's look at the New Age American churches. In these churches one must live in the present. *We--* reigning experts and leaders, especially bishops and priests, are *Christ, the Good Shepherd.* Just as "living tradition" has replaced Apostolic Tradition, so do clerics who have dethroned Christ replace Christ, the Good Shepherd. *We love you just as you are--*be you a prostitute, practicing homosexual, adulterer or any other sinner. *We care. We care* so much that we validate both you and your favorite politically correct sins. For example, we even give divorces. Of course, we label them annulments, but a divorce by any other name is still a divorce. Also, by way of an example, we--the upper clergy--love certain sins and sinful lifestyles so much that we spiritually rape or violate the modesty of children under our care by exposing them to the horrors of *sex education--American style.*

Since truth cannot be found in the past or in objective reality, there no longer exists a *God of revelation or of Catholic Tradition. Such a God is dead,* as Paul Tillich's disciple, William Alteizer, observed nearly forty years ago.

Effectively, man is God. Within each church body, reigning experts and authorities define *God,* or at least, spell out the parameters within which each can construct his own "God-idea." Each man can create *God, Jesus, Mary,* etc., as each decides. Each is free to be as charismaniacal as he desires--provided that he doesn't hold or propagate the faith or religion of our fathers--those who lived before 1960.

In many dioceses, at present, the Holy Sacrifice of the Mass has been replaced by a Eucharistic gathering, which celebrates man who is Christ among us. Christ's religion of the Canonized Mass as the Unbloody Sacrifice for our sins--has been discarded. Why? Man is not a sinner and needs *no Saviour.* In Christ, *all have been* (past tense) saved (if, of course, one felt such a need in the first place). In Christ, the salvation of humankind has been accomplished for all times and for all individuals. So teaches New Age Catholicism.

In such churches, each is considered to be sinless before God. *Confession* is *counseling.* No more does one go to Confession to have Mortal Sins forgiven by Christ through a valid priest in a valid sacrament. One goes to be *validated* or confirmed in his innate goodness and/or to be reconciled to man, the community.

New Age Catholicism teaches (in effect, if not actually) that man does not need God for forgiveness of sin or for the removal of guilt. In fact, as much as possible, reigning experts and authorities (at present) try to convince every Catholic that Original Sin or any of his favorite sins--homosexual acts, serial adultery, drunkenness, contracepting, and the like-- are no longer *really sins*. After all, how can any *man who is addressed as "Body of Christ" and who is the church,* be in any real danger of going to Hell-- unless, of course, he auto-excludes himself from Heaven, as the French Standard of the new Catechism of the Catholic Church (1992) teaches? (30 Days, Ratzinger, p. 48, No. 5, 1994)

What Tillich theorized and what Alteizer observed in the sixties has fully materialized in the nineties. Within many existential churches *God is dead.* Now, man is God. As such, he does not need forgiveness for sins. Just as he is baptized *not to wash away Original Sin but to enter the community,* likewise, he is validated or confirmed in his innate goodness by the community of man. Through the directive of the diabolically feminine modality in promoting man as god, New Age Catholicism increasingly accomplishes the replacement of traditional Catholicism with this alien concept.

IV. NEW AGE CATHOLICISM AND REIGNING EXPERTS IN THE NEW ORDER IMPOSE THE OTHER PHASE OF RUSSIA'S ERROR: THE DIABOLICALLY MASCULINE PHASE.

In the near future and increasingly in our present, reigning experts and authorities will tell you what is politely, politically, episcopally, presently, and positively *correct*. You must conform or be despised, and in some cases, deposed. For example, each parent who wants his child to be baptized, to receive First Holy Communion and to be confirmed *must attend* and be subjected to *biased indoctrination*, which is detrimental to his retaining and growing in the *Faith of his fathers*. Conform to New Age indoctrination or we'll punish your child! Sinfully scandalous sex ed is mandated for your child by your diocese. You as a parent must acquiesce and conform or remove your child from *their school.*

If you are a priest, you must conform or be punished--passed over for promotion, looked down upon, dismissed or worse. Each is brought into being or is treated as a dumbed-down conformist. The God-rejecting and man-affirming reigning experts and authorities *dominate* the dumbed-down masses as they decide. For example, *sacrilege in the hand* is edicted by reigning experts and authorities. Therefore, *all* must conform. Dare not any priest or *eucharistic minister* refuse to cooperate with *sacrilege in the hand.* Is it any wonder, there are so few priests?

THE NEW ORDER'S MOLDED SEMINARIANS

Let me give you a typical unwritten list of decrees which are strictly enforced in *all* diocesan (Novus Ordo) American seminaries. Each seminarian is raised to fit the present politically correct mold. He must conform or leave. The diabolically masculine modality has taken over seminary formation. What hope is there for our future?

A seminarian who believes as a true Catholic is considered to be inflexible, divisive, polemic, uncaring and regressive. He must be dismissed. A seminarian who believes in the Catholic Mass and Sacraments of the Traditional Church is to be dismissed. A seminarian must let the presently venerated experts determine his beliefs and opinions.

A seminarian must be effeminate or at least, he must be *positive to* women. He must work for and use *non-sexist language,* as presently defined by the reigning experts. He must *feel comfortable with women.* In some seminaries, he is even encouraged to date women. Any seminarian who looks upon girls negatively as temptations must be sent to a psychiatrist in order to be reprogrammed or he must be encouraged to leave.

A seminarian must be *other than God directed.* He must be a groupie. He must live to please others. He must perceive himself as a *facilitator* for others. A seminarian must see liturgy as the people's thing-- which *thing* is defined by reigning experts and authorities; and, at which *thing* he must be prepared to direct, coordinate or preside at: thankfully, properly, submissively, joyfully and lovingly. He must be (as Cardinal Ratzinger amusingly describes) an attractive *showmaster for a banal production.*

RE-CAP

The process is being implemented. That's the important thing to understand. This, briefly stated, is *the process*:

1) Deny each man's ability to know the Truth.

2) Affirm reigning experts and authorities as truth-givers.

3) Direct the masses--victims of reigning experts and authorities--to throw off any God-given basic negative convictions which would lead them back to *God as revealed.*

4) Direct the masses to rely on the *living* reigning experts and authorities for what is politically correct. Only the present politically correct view is to be tolerated.

TEMPORAL PROGNOSIS

If the pope doesn't activate the Fatima Opportunity, we will soon lose freedom and other temporal blessings in the USA. We will have to say bye-bye to the home of the free and the brave.

The next Olympics is scheduled for the man-centered year of 2000. Indeed, we *will not then* be celebrating two thousand years after Christ was born. If we were to celebrate this anniversary, we would have celebrated it in 1996 as scholars know.

Within the next few years, the princes of this world plan to bring about the New Order--both ecclesiastically and socially. The two beasts plan to reign--or, at least, begin their New World Order (Novus Ordo Seclorum) in spirit, if not also in fact.

If the beasts succeed, Americans will wistfully look back at 1996. It was the last year when one could honestly sing *"the land of the free and the home of the brave"* at the World Olympics.

The New World leaders plan to ban national competitions in favor of individual competitions in a world devoid of *conflict agents--nations, negative religions, private possessions, and similar "non-communistic" factors.* These plans were mirrored in the opening tableau (or the opening prayer service). *"Imagine..."* was sung. Imagine no Hell, no religion, no private property, etc. Then--and only then--the world will live as one. Also, throughout the Olympic broadcast, we were assured over and over again, that *we are the global community.*

Unless the Fatima Opportunity is properly activated, we will soon be totally under Russia's Error--the enthronement of man and the dethronement of *God as revealed. The land of the free and the home of the brave* will be replaced with a village or a *community dictatorially ruled by fear and force.*

BRINGING HOME MY POINT

We who watched these Olympics unfold on television were given a prelude to our temporal future as the life of a Chinese gymnast was presented. *From the age of eight, she was taken from her parents and given to the State.* In this long period of time she visited her parents only once.

What did her parents fearfully and *unnaturally* confess? *"We were glad to give our child to China."* They were glad to give their child to the community. They rejoiced in giving their child to the village. Wake up to this horror which comes from our living under the Fatima Curse.

What, if on prime television, the parent of a fourteen year old said, *"We were glad to give our eight year old to God and send her to a cloistered convent"?* Do you begin to see how we've rejected God and enthroned man--especially the *community*?

Perhaps for the last time in Olympic history, a great heroine (Kerri Struggs) represented the land of the free and the brave. It was the last vault exercise. She was the very last to vault. She was the last hope for team USA *getting the gold.* It all depended on her. She failed to properly land on her feet after the first vault. It looked like the USA would wind up with the silver or the bronze. Then, in pain, she limped back to start her second vault. We all thought *"Quit now, you can't do better and you'll hurt yourself even more."* Her coach encouraged her to try again. However, it remained *her decision*--not the decision of the ecclesial or national or world community.

She was one of the *free and the brave*. She was free to decide. Love could motivate her--love of parents, of her coach, of herself or even of God. Being free, she could choose to be *brave*. As enslaved she would only be able to conform or to suffer. She was the epitome of free and brave. Her right foot was so injured that, on her second vault, she *fixed her landing on one foot* with the injured one giving her an assist. Then she raised her hands indicating completion and fell to the floor in extreme pain.

She reminded me of our former heroine, Nadia Comaneche of Romania. In a television interview Nadia gave us a preview of coming horrors. She defected from the New Age or the New World Order (which was then largely confined to Russia and its enslaved territories). Nadia cited a reason I'll never forget. She didn't want to live in a continual state of *fear of man*.

In *community-run* Romania, one *feared the community* so much that he feared going out of the doorway with the right foot leading, lest a law existed demanding one lead with his left. That's the actual example she cited.

Ridiculous? That's your future unless enough pray and "suffer for God" so that the pope will be graced to properly activate the Fatima Opportunity. On that day of Consecration, the bishops of the world, along with the pope, will confess their sins, repent and then vow reparation of the *only hope of mankind*--the Catholic Church, *outside of which there exists no salvation.*

It's all up to you--to personally conquer the Novus Ordo Seclorum, by God's inspirations and graces; and to pray, suffer and act *so as to bring about the Marian Pope* who will obey God's Fatima Command, and thus the Pope who will bring us into the era of Fatima Blessings--an era within which each will live in freedom from man and his reign of ruthless tyranny.

THE ETERNAL PROGNOSIS OF INFINITE WORTH

We abide under the curse from Original Sin as well as under the Fatima Curse. Today, the demons are very successful. They lead into awesome darkness. Worst of all, they lead many souls into eternal Hell.

Many of us fail to perceive and live with the conviction of each individual's eternal and infinite worth, and thus of the infinite importance of this life. Many live in awesome darkness--indifferent to the eternal and infinite life that will be ours after death. They know neither themselves nor their Creator, Lord and Judge. In His merciful love towards some of us, God has bestowed knowledge and conviction of the awesome Fatima Message.

This God-given message assures us that we are in one of the most cursed times in history. God assures us that we abide within a grossly dysfunctional existential church. He gives us this assurance not only through His Fatima Message, but also through the words of certain popes and saints.

POPES FORESAW THE FATIMA CURSE

A few popes foresaw and dreaded the Fatima Curse. Pope Gregory XVI envisaged this apocalyptic scene in 1834.

> We say, in truth, that the pit of the abyss is open, from where St. John saw smoke arise up that darkened the sun and locusts came forth and invaded the extension of the earth...We are horrified, venerable brethren, at seeing with what doctrines, or better said, with what monster of errors we find ourselves buried in. (Pope Gregory XVI, 1834)

Nearly fifty years later, Pope Leo XIII, in ecstasy after saying his Tridentine Mass, saw Satan unleashed. This great pope also perceived the *evil spirit* which would be loosed during this time.

> These most crafty enemies have filled and inebriated with gall and bitterness the Church, the spouse of the Immaculate Lamb, and have laid impious hands on her most sacred possessions. In the Holy Place itself, where has been set up the See of the most holy Peter and the Chair of Truth for the Light of the world, they have raised the throne of their abominable impiety, with the

iniquitous design that when the Pastor has been struck, the sheep may be scattered. (The Raccolta, Benziger Brothers, 1930, 314-315)

Pope Saint Pius X foretold the approaching Fatima Curse. He saw it coming. Here are his exact words-- words which predicted the Fatima Curse that, less than 15 years later, would be confirmed and addressed by God and His Mother in the Fatima Message as Russia's Errors. With the authority of a pope and saint, Pope St. Pius X perceives this curse to be *"man substitutes himself for God."* That which is called *Russia's Errors* by Our Lady and *this monstrous and detestable iniquity* by Pope Pius X, is the same abomination which I label Russia's Error.

We understood that it belonged to Us, in virtue of the pontifical office entrusted to Us, to provide a remedy for such a great evil [apostasy from God]. We believed that this order of God was addressed to Us: 'Behold, today I set you over nations and kingdoms, to tear down and destroy, to build up and to plant.' (Jer 1, 10) ...It is necessary, by every means, and at the price of any effort, to uproot entirely *this monstrous and detestable iniquity proper to the times we are living in, and through which man substitutes himself for God...*Truly, whoever ponders these things must necessarily and firmly fear whether such a perversion of minds is not the sign announcing, and the beginning of the last times, and that the Son of Perdition spoken of by the Apostle (II Thess 2, 3) might already be living on this earth.

So great is the audacity and so great the rage with which religion is mocked everywhere, and the dogmas of the faith are fought against, there is a stubborn effort to completely suppress man's duties towards God! Now, this, according to the same Apostle, is the character proper to Antichrist: man, with unspeakable temerity, has usurped the place of the Creator, lifting himself above everything that bears the name of God. It has reached such a point that, being powerless to completely extinguish in himself the notion of God, he nevertheless shakes off the yoke of His Majesty, and dedicates the visible world to himself in the guise of the temple, where he pretends to receive the adoration of his own kind. "He sits in the temple of God, and gives himself out as if he were God" (II Thess 2, 4). (Pope Pius X)

God knows all. Through His Mother, He also disclosed or predicted the negative attitude that popes (from Pius XI on) would take to the God-given Fatima Opportunity. Our Lady thus commented to Sister Lucy in a vision she received in 1931:

> Tell my ministers [the popes] who behave like the King of France by procrastinating in carrying out my wishes, that they will follow him into suffering the same misfortune. It is never too late to have recourse to Jesus and Mary...Like the King of France, they will regret it and will do it, even though [in the case of the pope] late.(The Whole Truth About Fatima, Frere Michael, brackets mine)

How late depends on the pope. How late depends on you and me, since God assured us at Fatima that when a sufficient number of us are praying and sacrificing for the pope, He will overwhelmingly grace the pope into activating the Fatima Opportunity. In the meantime, let us strive to realize the fact that we live under the Fatima Curse. We do so in order to be greatly motivated to pray and sacrifice *so as to bring into existence* the Marian Pope of our times. To help us to be motivated to act, we contemplate the dire warnings of Pope Pius XII.

Pope Pius XII, according to Msgr. Roche, writing in Pie devant l'histoire, dreaded the coming of a bad pope as well as of a *false mass*. Has not a false Mass materialized? Have not recent popes been bad--in

154

that they have failed to activate the Fatima Opportunity and have failed to properly or plenarily "pope"?

A day will come when the civilized world will deny its God, when the Church will doubt, as Peter doubted. She will be tempted to believe that man has become God...in our churches Christians will search in vain for the red lamp where God awaits them. Like Magdalen weeping before the empty tomb, they will ask 'Where have they taken Him?' (pp. 52-53).

Also, within these Fatima times, we note that Pope Paul VI observed that the smoke of Satan had entered the sanctuary of the Church. Sanctuary smoke is smoke of worship. Was Pope Paul VI honestly commenting on his *non-infallibly decreed* creation--the Novus Ordo, as being the *abominable desolation set up in the sanctuary,* as predicted by God's prophet (Dn 11:31)? Does the Novus Ordo *as it exists in its many different expressions* fulfill the prediction made by all of the Church Fathers that *there would come a time when the Holy Sacrifice will cease?*

At the beginning of his pontificate, Pope John Paul

II met with the German bishops at Fulda. They persisted in uncovering the Third Revelation of Fatima, which was kept secret by papal command.

Pope John Paul evaded the question. Finally, after disclosing awesome horrors that are in store for us, he desperately urged them: "Pray the rosary. Pray the rosary."

This reminds us of a prophecy given by Our Lady of Fatima that a time will come when "all that you will have is *the rosary and devotion to my Immaculate Heart.*" It would seem that we must first bottom out before things can be turned around. Also, from Our Lady's words, it would seem that when we bottom out, there will be very few--if any--valid Masses, as predicted by all of the Church Fathers.

THE SUN REPARED

We live within a time of awesome temptations. *Many many go to eternal Hell.* However, we do not live without hope--hope that a time will come when many will be saved from eternal Hell, a time when the establishment church will be repared.

At Fatima, after Our Lady intervened, the sun was repared. The *rainbow of peace* indicates that the Church will be repared. As Fatima promises and as John Bosco confirms, this sun will shine so brightly that it will convert Russia to Catholicism and will bring many souls into Heaven. The one and only Church of Christ will be spectacularly repared!

Over the whole world, there will appear a sun as bright as the flames of the Cenacle, such as will never be seen from that time until the end of time
(The Memoires, St. John Bosco)

Our hope for the future comes from our realizing the fact that we live under the Fatima Curse, thereby becoming motivated to accept and implement the God-given Fatima Message, the message of hope.

On October 13, 1917, in Fatima, everyone saw the sun--representing the existential church--being not only *totally dysfunctional*, but also a grave menace to mankind. *Some saw the cross leaving the sun.* Did this mean that Christ's Sacrifice would leave the existential church?

The sun, representing the existential church, was *aberrant and dysfunctional*. It left its appointed orbit or function, pleased men with various colorations, and finally, it became so dysfunctional that it became the scourge of mankind and was about to destroy all mankind. Then, the Immaculata, by the power given to her by God, restored or repared the existential church. She restored the sun to its par or to its proper functioning.

Indeed, as Fatima disclosed, Our Lady is God's freely chosen prime end-times sacramental. Through her, ecclesial reparation will materialize. The sun will become brighter than ever before.

In the light of what we have stated, St. John Bosco's prophecy is even more foreboding:

> Your sons ask for bread of faith and no one gives it to them...Ungrateful Rome, effeminate Rome, arrogant Rome...forgetting that the Sovereign Pontiff's and your true glory are on Golgotha...Woe to you. My Law is an idle word for you. (The Memoires, St. John Bosco)

"Your true glory is on Golgotha." We should glory in the Holy Sacrifice of the Mass. However, has not there come a time when the pope/Rome axis no longer glories in the Holy Sacrifice on Golgotha as

coming to us in an unbloody way in the Holy Sacrifice of the Mass?

WHICH MASS WILL ECCLESIAL REPARATION REQUIRE?

De facto, an ever increasing number of those who are actively devoted to the fulfillment of the Fatima request are *converting* to the Canonized [Tridentine] Mass Liturgy, especially, among the clergy. Is the link between the two--Fatima evangelization and devotion to the Canonized [Tridentine] Mass Liturgy--coincidental or providential?

The Third Secret most likely discloses the Fatima challenge: the existential church must confess its own horrible condition, repent and be repared or restored. Must not the existential church return to being that which it has rejected or disowned--the *semper ubique idem* (always and everywhere the same) Church of nineteen centuries--in order to bring about the conversion of Russia? Otherwise, to what will Russia be converted?

Understating the obvious, even Pope Paul VI, on several occasions, confessed that the (incense) smoke of Satan was in our sanctuaries. What is supposed to happen within our sanctuaries? The Holy Sacrifice of the Mass is supposed to happen within Catholic sanctuaries. Does not the *Novus Ordo as said* sacrilege the Sacrifice? Most confess that a meal has replaced the Sacrifice. Nearly all (80% of those under age 55 in the USA) reject the Catholic Eucharistic dogma. Over 50% of priests in North America don't believe in transubstantiation. How can these priests say valid Masses? Does not sacrilege result? Is not Satan rather than God, worshiped within Novus Ordo sanctuaries, as even Pope Paul VI confessed?

While consecrating the world (*not Russia*) on March 25, 1984, Pope John Paul II confessed that the people (of Russia) were still awaiting their consecration (at some future date). Cardinal Ratzinger, along with other curial cardinals, declared that the infamous consecration (March 25, 1984) *was not the Fatima Consecration demanded by God.* (Fatima Crusader, March 1988)

How can this be the era of Fatima Blessings when this same cardinal confessed that the reigning *new order church was built on lies and half-truths?* If, as some contend, new church is old and true

Catholicism, why then, is the Tridentine Mass forbidden and even hated by most prelates? From observation of how new church treats the devoted disciples of old Church, we are led to conclude that two different religions or two opposing churches exist. To which church or religion, do you think God is calling us? Which church or religion will be *the Church* in that great era of Fatima blessing?

Many other relevant questions can be posited. However, let these suffice for indicating appropriate areas of inquiry in order to resolve the question as to which church or religion will constitute the era of Fatima Blessing. To which church or religion will Russia convert?

The God-given Fatima Message, initially (in 1916), focused on the Eucharist, as obtained from a Tridentine Mass. Will not the Church of the Tridentine Mass be *the vehicle used by God to convert Russia?*

Did not Our Lady command that a church wherein the Tridentine Mass would be said should be built at Fatima, as well as at all of her other popular shrines? Did not the climacteric vision of Fatima--the Great Salutary Theophany at Tuy--illustrate and confirm that the Tridentine Mass was the Holy Sacrifice of Christ from which all salutary graces flowed?

De facto, all Church-approved Marian apparitions have been associated with the Canonical (Tridentine) Mass. (See my book, Holy Mary Holy Mass.) *"In this Holy Mass are contained all the fruits and graces which the Son of God poured on the Church"*--St. Thomas.

Is the reparation or restoration of the Tridentine Liturgy as *par* or canon part of the Fatima Blessings? Was curial Cardinal Silvio Oddi correct in stating that *"The suppression of the Latin Mass is a crime for which history will never forgive the church"?*

If he and others of like mind are correct, then the restoration of the Tridentine Mass will be a major sign as well as a major part of repentance and reparation. Is not restitution expected for this *crime committed against Our Lady, Jesus and the Holy Trinity?* Is not the restoration of the Canonized Mass part of *the blessing for which history will always thank the Church*--part of this ecclesial restitution to Christ and His Church of all times and places? Is not the reparation or full restoration of the Canonized Mass an essential part of the Fatima Blessing? Honest answers to questions such as these at least emphasize the urgency of our praying, sacrificing and working to bring about the God-promised era of Fatima Blessings.

What will result when a pope activates the Fatima Opportunity? Russia will be converted to Catholicism. The world will be at peace. Such a peace will exist as dogmatically defined by popes before 1958. The era of peace will materialize under the reign of Christ the King, and herald the reign of authentic Catholicism throughout the world.

LEARNING FROM THE PAST

Every period of ecclesial crisis has called forth a papal resolution--either by a dogmatic and binding decree or through a pope-approved dogmatic council, the last of which was Vatican I. We can expect the same pattern to materialize in the near future.

The era of Fatima Blessing--which the Marian Pope of modern times will initiate--will call forth many dogmatic decrees. Why? The Catholic Church, which is the only means of salvation, must be repared in order that Russia be converted and in order that many will be saved.

What will be dogmatically decreed? We can expect many practical issues--from ecumenism to liturgy--to be resolved when the upper clergy, under the pope, embrace the God-given Fatima Opportunity.

Until fiducial or moral crises are dogmatically resolved, freedom within the parameters of binding past dogmas prevails, and each must properly inform, form and then follow his own conscience. For the sake of your eternal well-being, please accept the ecclesially embarrassing Fatima Message It's our only hope. Only if enough of us become convinced of its awesome necessity to be implemented will the era of Fatima Blessing materialize.

When (not if) the Fatima Opportunity receives a positive response--then Russia will be converted to Catholicism; and, of infinite and eternal importance, many will be saved from eternal Hell--instead of many going to Hell, as prevails while we remain under the Fatima Curse. Then, in place of Russia's Error evangelizing and imprisoning the world, we will have the reign of Christ the King: in place of wars in various places throughout the world, we will enjoy world peace--the peace that only Christ can give.

At Fatima, God gave His Mother as His freely chosen prime end-times sacramental. If we do as she says, God will turn the Fatima Curse into the Fatima Blessing. It's all up to the pope--and--it's all up to you and me. When enough are sufficiently praying and sacrificing, then God will overwhelmingly grace the pope into activating the Fatima Opportunity.

RUSSIA'S ERROR

OTHER TITLES
by
Fr. Paul Trinchard, S.T.L.

ALL ABOUT SALVATION
APOSTASY WITHIN
THE AWESOME FATIMA CONSECRATION
HOLY MARY HOLY MASS
NEW AGE NEW MASS
NEW MASS IN LIGHT OF THE OLD
MY BASIC MISSAL
THE MASS THAT MADE PADRE PIO

RUSSIA'S ERROR $12.00

Ask about our bulk prices.

Write for a catalog.

MAETA
PO Box 6012
METAIRIE LA 70009-6012